LAUNCH YOUR FIRST AI BUSINESS IN 20 DAYS

TABLE OF CONTENTS

INTRODUCTION

Hi and Welcome!

If you're holding this book, then somewhere deep down, you're dreaming of starting your own business—or maybe you're already on the edge of making it real. Either way, congratulations. You've already taken the first (and sometimes hardest) step.

WHAT THIS BOOK IS—AND ISN'T

This is not a book that promises you'll get rich overnight.

It's not one of those "just copy this and make millions" guides. It won't guarantee you'll pick the perfect product on your first try. And no, just reading it won't make sales magically roll in while you lie on the beach. But putting it into action? Step by step? That's where the real magic starts to happen.

Here's what this book will do:

It will walk you step-by-step through the process of creating your very first digital product and building a real online presence around it.

It will teach you how to use AI tools (without needing to be tech-savvy) to brainstorm, design, write, promote, and sell in ways that feel good—not salesy.

It will show you how to build something that lasts—a brand that reflects you, and a store that grows alongside your creativity.

And most importantly? If you show up and put in the effort, this book can help you take your first meaningful steps toward independence. Maybe it won't replace your day job today. But the goal is for you to start—and to keep building until it can.

Whether you've got one hour a week or one hour a day, you'll find real progress here—because this isn't about rushing. It's about creating something you care about, at a pace that's sustainable, and learning as you go.

Each day includes:

- A practical, no-fluff lesson written in plain, clear and simple language
  - Clear explanations of tools and techniques (AI and beyond)
  - Practice prompts and daily checklists
  - A space for your personal notes, reflections, and edits

You can go day by day, or you can pause when you need more time. This is your book. Use it how it works best for you.

You Might Not Get It Right the First Time—and That's Okay

This is your launchpad. Not your finish line.

Your first product may not be a 10/10. That's normal. The goal isn't perfection—it's momentum. Because the more you create, the better you'll get. The more you test, the more you'll learn. And eventually? You'll have something you're incredibly proud of.

So take your time. Highlight what matters. Come back to the tough spots. And above all, try the things. You'll grow through doing—not just reading.

ABOUT THE AUTHOR: WHY I WROTE THIS

Hi, I'm Tessa Quinn Rae. I've been working in IT for over 15 years. I started out in customer support, and over the years—with a lot of curiosity, effort, and trial and error—I moved into a director-level role where I now oversee both engineering and procurement teams. I work closely with sales, marketing, and operations, and I genuinely love what I do.

But I'm also a creator.

Outside of work, I run my own online business — I sell digital products under several brands on platforms like Etsy and Amazon. This book? It's one of those products—but it's also deeply personal. It's built on lived experience, real trial and error, and the messiness of figuring things out while juggling all the other things life throws at you—like most of us do.

Even with all my years in IT—and having access to engineers, developers, and tech experts—I still struggled when I started out. So if you're not technical, if all of this feels overwhelming at first, know that you're not alone. And that's exactly why I wrote this— to make it less intimidating, more doable, and a little bit more human.

I wrote it because I remember how hard it was to get started. To figure things out with no clear path, bouncing between YouTube videos, blog posts, and trial-and-error experiments that sometimes went nowhere.

This guide is the book I wish I had back then.

And it's one I can write now because I've seen both sides—corporate and creative, structured and scrappy. I use AI daily in my job to simplify and speed up everything from planning to communication. I also use it in my business to design, brainstorm, organize, and automate.

I believe anyone—with the right tools, mindset, and just enough permission to try before they feel ready—can build something online that reflects who they are and makes money. Even if you're working a full-time job. Even if you're at home raising little ones. Even if you're just figuring it all out as you go.

This book is my way of sharing what I've learned—and giving you a boost so you don't have to start from zero like I did.

So here's my advice:

- Don't rush it. This isn't a race.
- Don't skip the practice work. That's where the learning sticks.
- And don't be afraid to get messy. Messy is good. Messy means you're trying.

You'll find a daily checklist at the end of each section. Use it. Make notes. Track what worked, what didn't, and what you changed. Treat this book like your own personal workspace.

And when you're ready to launch your second product? You'll already have a map.

Now, take a pencil, grab your highlighters, and let's figure out how to launch your online business—one real, doable step at a time.

WEEK 1:

AI FOUNDATION + FAST WINS

Hey there! Welcome to Day 1. If you're holding this book, that means you're either ready—or dreaming—of launching your own business. Well, congratulations. You've already made it one step closer to making that goal a reality.

Today, we're setting the stage for your 20-day journey into making real income with the help of AI. We're not here to pack your brain with theory—we're going to do the thing, together.

Let's start by getting everything in place. Imagine you're about to cook a new dish—you wouldn't want to realize halfway through that you're missing some ingredients. Same goes for your AI tools. Getting your setup done today means fewer delays later.

You might be wondering: "Should I wait to sign up until I understand each tool?". Totally fair question—but here's why we're doing this now:

- **You'll move faster when nothing's blocking you**. Set it and forget it—for now.

- **These tools will be used often.** We won't repeat setup steps later. You're building your foundation.

- **This is a mindset shift.** Signing up and logging in says, "I'm doing this for real."

And don't stress if something on the list looks unfamiliar. You don't need to be tech-savvy—we'll go through how and why to use each one as we go. Right now, your job is just to get the doors open. We'll explore the rooms together soon.

TOOLS YOU'LL NEED

Most of these are free or have generous free versions. I'm not affiliated with any of them—I don't earn commissions if you sign up. These are simply the tools I use daily in my own business, and what I believe are the best balance of beginner-friendly and powerful. There's a printable with all the tool names and links via a QR code at the end of the book if you want to revisit them later.

- **ChatGPT** (or **Gemini** / **Claude**) – for brainstorming, scripting, and   planning.
  (Free with optional upgrades)
- **Canva** – for design work (graphics, mockups, printables).
  (Free, with Pro tier)
- **DALL·E** or **Midjourney** – to generate images.
  (DALL·E: limited free; Midjourney: paid subscription)
- **Printify** / **Printful** / **Gelato** – for selling physical items via print-on-demand.
  (Free, charges per product sold)
- **Etsy** or **Gumroad** – to list and sell your products.
  (Etsy has small listing fees; Gumroad starts free).

Hold on with this one if you are unsure which one to use, we'll discuss the options later in the book.

- **Notion** / **Google Docs** / **Evernote** – for organizing your plans,   content,   and   progress.
  (All have free tiers)
- **Pinterest** + **Google Trends** – to research what people are looking   for.
  (Both free)

Note: I highly recommend reading the Terms and Conditions for each service you plan to use. It's okay if you can't do it on day one, but please set aside time before going live with your business to understand how your content, data or designs might be used or stored.

About Store Setup:

Etsy will ask you to name your store during sign-up. If you don't have the perfect name yet—no worries. Choose something general that reflects your niche. Think "Mom Planner Co" or "Cozy Prints Studio." You can rename your Etsy shop later, but only once without needing special approval, so make it flexible.

Gumroad doesn't require a formal store name during initial setup—you'll create a username that acts as your shop link (like gumroad.com/yourname), and this can be changed at any time. Your display name and product pages are customizable later, so there's no pressure to finalize anything today.

The goal today is just to have your accounts ready so you're not held back when it's time to launch.

BROWSER EXTENSIONS TO INSTALL

These aren't required—but they'll streamline your process a lot. Most are free and take less than a minute to install.

- o **Grammarly** – helps clean up your writing for product listings, posts, emails, and descriptions.
  (Free and paid plans)

o **ChatGPT for Google** – shows quick AI responses right in your search results.
  (Free)
o **Save to Notion / Evernote** Web Clipper – lets you save useful links, images, or ideas you come across.
  (Free)
o **Pinterest** Save Button – quickly pin things to your boards.
  (Free)
o **ColorZilla** – lets you grab color codes from websites—great for keeping branding consistent.
  (Free)

Not sure how ColorZilla helps? Imagine seeing a shade you love on another shop or Pinterest. You can instantly grab that hex code and use it in Canva to match your product or brand color scheme.

Prioritize installing Grammarly and ChatGPT for Google first. They'll instantly boost your writing and research.

YOUR WORKSPACE HUB

You need a space to plan, organize, and capture ideas. Here are your best bets:

o **Google Docs /** Notion – for writing, saving prompts, notes, and   outlines
  (Google Docs: Free with a Google account; Notion: Free for personal use)

- **Evernote** – for design inspiration or screenshots *(Free basic plan (limited sync and uploads), with paid upgrades)*
- **Smartsheet** – for creating Gantt charts and deadlines *(Free limited version available; full features require a paid plan)*
- **Bookmark** Folder – create a folder in your browser named "AI Biz" or whatever feels right to you. Start saving your go-to tools, marketplaces, and references in one place. *(Totally free and built into your browser)*

You don't need anything fancy to stay organized—just a space where everything lives. This could be a Notion dashboard, a Google Doc or Smartsheet, or even a physical notebook if you're more old-school. The goal is to keep track of ideas for products and content; notes on what you're learning; links to useful tools, trends, and references and daily goals and accomplishments.

If you're using Notion, you can create a dashboard with sections like "Ideas", "In Progress", "To Publish" and "Launched". For Google Docs, just make one doc with headers or a table to organize everything.

This workspace will grow with you. Keep it open while you work—you'll find yourself jotting things down all the time. It's your creative hub, and it'll make a huge difference in staying focused and feeling in control.

In my business I use Google Docs and Notepad to track product ideas, Smartsheet for planning and deadlines, Pinterest and

Evernote for inspiration. I also keep a doc of articles and resources I want to study before launching a new phase.

Before we wrap up today, take a moment to breathe and appreciate the fact that you've already made your first move. Most people never get this far. You've just said yes to a new way of working and earning—and that's a big deal.

Tomorrow, we'll dive into the heart of it all: **prompts**. You'll learn how to talk to AI in a way that gets you powerful results. No coding, no jargon—just clear steps that you can use right away. See you there!

WHAT YOU'VE LEARNED TODAY

Today you've laid the groundwork for everything that's coming next. You picked and set up the tools that will support your creative and business journey, from brainstorming and design to mockups and organization. You installed smart browser extensions, created your first productivity workspace, and took real action toward building your AI-powered income stream. It might not feel flashy, but this kind of setup is what turns ideas into momentum. And you've officially begun.

DAY 1: SETUP CHECKLIST

- ☐ Create accounts for:
- ☐ ChatGPT (or Gemini / Claude)
- ☐ Canva
- ☐ DALL·E or Midjourney
- ☐ Printify, Printful, or Gelato
- ☐ Etsy or Gumroad
- ☐ Notion / Google Docs / Evernote
- ☐ Install browser tools:
- ☐ Grammarly
- ☐ ChatGPT for Google
- ☐ Save to Notion or Evernote Web Clipper
- ☐ Pinterest Save Button
- ☐ ColorZilla
- ☐ Get organized:
  - ☐ Create a digital (or physical) workspace to track product ideas, tasks, and content
  - ☐ Organize a folder system for images and filesCreate a bookmarks folder in your browser for quick access to tools and resources

DAY 2: MASTERING PROMPTS

Welcome to Day 2! Today we're diving into one of the most valuable skills you'll pick up in this journey—learning how to get what you need from AI tools just by asking the right way. Think of this like learning how to ask great questions, because that's really what prompts are.

When you use tools like ChatGPT, Midjourney, or others, the results you get depend almost entirely on how you ask. It's not about being clever or technical—it's about being clear. If you've ever asked a question and gotten a totally weird or useless answer, that's probably because the prompt didn't give enough direction.

Today, we'll take the guesswork out of it. You'll learn:

- How to ask better questions (aka prompts) that give you useful answers
- How to get ideas, outlines, or visuals in the style you want
- How to tweak the tone or format of AI responses so they sound more "you"
- A few quick templates that will save you time and brainpower

By the end of the day, you'll know how to guide the AI instead of crossing your fingers and hoping it figures it out. Let's get into it.

WHAT IS A PROMPT AND WHY IT MATTERS

So, what exactly is a prompt? It's just a message you type to an AI tool to tell it what you want. That's it. Think of it like asking a friend for a favor: the more clearly you explain what you need, the better chance you have of getting something helpful in return.

If you give a half-baked request, you'll usually get a half-baked result. But if you take a moment to think about what you really want—what tone, what format, how much detail—you'll usually get something surprisingly good.

The cool part? You don't need to be a writer or use fancy words. You just need to get comfortable giving clear directions.

Let me show you what I mean:

Not-so-great prompt:

> *WRITE SOMETHING ABOUT MUGS*

Much better prompt:

> *GIVE ME THREE SHORT AND FUNNY SLOGANS FOR A COFFEE MUG, AIMED AT BUSY MOMS. KEEP THE TONE PLAYFUL AND RELATABLE.*

Same topic, totally different vibe. The second one tells the AI what you're actually looking for—and that's where the magic happens.

In the next section, we'll look at a few go-to styles you can keep using anytime you need a solid result, fast. These aren't rules—they're more like recipes that work really well, especially when you're just just starting to get the hang of things.

Think of these like fill-in-the-blank starters. You can copy, tweak, and reuse them whenever you want.

1. Role + Task + Tone

Ask the AI to step into a role, give it a task, and tell it how to sound.

> *YOU ARE A PRODUCT DESCRIPTION WRITER. CREATE A SHORT, FUN ETSY LISTING FOR A MUG WITH THE PHRASE "MOM FUEL". KEEP THE TONE LIGHT AND PLAYFUL.*

2. Act Like X

Great for writing styles or specific voices.

> *ACT LIKE A SASSY BEST FRIEND. GIVE ME 5 BOLD CAPTIONS FOR A T-SHIRT THAT SAYS "TOO TIRED TO CARE.*

3. Give Me Options

Perfect when you're brainstorming.

> *I'M DESIGNING A CAP FOR DOG LOVERS. GIVE ME 10 SHORT SLOGAN IDEAS, RANGING FROM SWEET TO FUNNY.*

4. Rewrite or Expand This

Use this when you have a rough idea but want it improved.

> *REWRITE THIS TO SOUND MORE EXCITING: "THIS CUP KEEPS DRINKS HOT"*

5. Break It Down

Great for outlines, lists, or step-by-step tasks.

> *BREAK DOWN THE STEPS TO CREATE A CUSTOMER WELCOME EXPERIENCE AFTER SOMEONE BUYS A PRODUCT FROM MY ETSY STORE*

You don't need to memorize these—just start practicing and you'll find your favorites. You can even keep your own little "Prompt Bank" in Notion or your notes app.

PRACTICE: YOUR TURN

Let's put what you've learned into action. Below are a few prompts you can test out for yourself. You'll want to use a tool like ChatGPT, Claude, or Gemini—whichever one you've signed up for on Day 1. Just open it in a browser tab, copy one of the prompts below, paste it in, and hit enter.

As you try things out, you'll see how the AI reacts to whatever you throw at it. Sometimes it'll get it just right, other times it might be a bit off—and that's totally okay. You can always tweak the wording, shift the vibe, or take another stab with a new prompt. This is how you start building your feel for what works.

Pick one or two of these and give them a shot:

1. Brainstorm a product

YOU ARE AN ETSY SELLER. SUGGEST 10 PRINT-ON-DEMAND MUG IDEAS FOR TEACHERS THAT WOULD SELL WELL IN SPRING

2. Create a slogan

ACT LIKE A WITTY COPYWRITER. COME UP WITH 5 PLAYFUL SLOGANS FOR A TOTE BAG ABOUT BOOK LOVERS

3. Build a product description

WRITE A SHORT AND FUN DESCRIPTION FOR A DAD HAT THAT SAYS "FUELED BY COFFEE & CHAOS"

4. Outline a process

> *BREAK DOWN THE STEPS TO TURN CUSTOMER*
> *FEEDBACK INTO A SOCIAL MEDIA POST OR STORY*
> *THAT BUILDS TRUST AND ENGAGEMENT*

5. Tweak something you've written

> *REWRITE THIS TO SOUND MORE CONFIDENT: "I*
> *THINK THIS MIGHT WORK FOR PEOPLE WHO LIKE*
> *CUTE STUFF"*

Try them out and see what feels natural to you. You're not aiming for perfection—just progress. Think of it like sketching: the more you do it, the better your instincts get.

WHAT YOU'VE LEARNED TODAY

Let's take a moment to look back on what you covered today.

You learned that prompts are the way you guide AI—it can only give you good results if it gets clear direction from you. The more specific you are, the better it responds.

A helpful way to write prompts is to think in simple terms: who do you want the AI to act like, what do you want it to do, and what tone should it use? That small shift makes prompting a lot easier.

Even just a few minutes of practice a day can go a long way. You'll start to notice your confidence growing—and your results improving—faster than you might expect.

Tomorrow, we'll change gears. With your tools set up, it's time to roll up your sleeves and start building real digital products. We're taking your ideas and turning them into something people actually want. Let's get to it.

DAY 2: LEARN PROMPTING CHECKLIST

☐ Try 2–3 prompt variations in ChatGPT (or Gemini / Claude)

☐ Write and test a simple product description

☐ Practice rewriting or expanding something you've written

☐ Save your favorite prompts somewhere you can reuse them

☐ Create your own Prompt Bank (Google Doc, Notion page, or Notes app)

☐ Brainstorm 10 print-on-demand mug ideas using a prompt

☐ Write 5 playful slogans using the 'Act like' prompt framework

☐ Draft a short product description using a prompt of your own

☐ Break down a process using the 'Outline a process' style

☐ Note what felt easy or confusing—track what you'd like to practice more

DAY 3: CREATING DIGITAL PRODUCTS

Welcome to Day 3! Today is about getting something out of your head and into the world. If you've ever thought, "I'm not creative enough", or "Where would I even start?"—you're not alone. The good news? You don't need to be a designer or a writer. You just need a little direction and the tools you already set up.

By the end of today, you'll have your very first digital product. Maybe it's a printable checklist, a journaling page, or a simple guide—whatever it is, it'll be yours, and it'll be ready to sell.

WHAT CAN YOU MAKE?

Let's not overcomplicate things. Here are some digital products that are quick to create and work well for platforms like Etsy or Gumroad. You don't have to choose from this list—you're always welcome to go with an idea of your own. Think of these as test runs: you can start with one of these, learn the ropes, spot a few mistakes, and then confidently create product #2—something closer to your original vision, only with less guesswork and more experience under your belt.

- Printable planners and checklist
- Simple wall art
- Coloring pages (great for both kids and adults)
- Mini how-to guides or eBooks

You only need one idea to start. This isn't about being perfect—it's about getting something out there.

STEP 1: COME UP WITH A PRODUCT IDEA

Open ChatGPT (or Gemini / Claude) and try something like:

> *GIVE ME 10 BEGINNER-FRIENDLY DIGITAL PRODUCT IDEAS THAT WOULD SELL WELL ON ETSY THIS SPRING. FOCUS ON MOMS, TEACHERS, STUDENTS*

(or whoever you want to target your products for)

Skim the ideas it gives you. Pick one that feels doable and fun. Don't overthink it. Pick one and roll with it.

Once you've picked your idea, run a quick search on Etsy or Pinterest to see if there's already demand. You're not looking for something brand-new—instead, you want signs that people are already buying things like it. Because no matter how great your product is—if nobody wants it, it won't sell. Or at the very least, it'll require time, money, and effort to convince people they need it.

Here's what to look for:

Use Etsy's Search and Autocomplete

Start typing your idea into Etsy's search bar. The autocomplete suggestions are based on real searches—if your idea shows up, people are actively looking for it. Try a few keyword variations to see what pops up. If nothing appears, it might be too niche (or just not in demand).

Scan Listings for Demand Hints

Click into a few top listings. Look for:

- High shop sales numbers
- Recent reviews (especially if people mention the product directly)
- Etsy's "Bestseller" tag, which indicates strong and steady sales

Use Free and Paid Research Tools

These tools estimate demand and help you compare niches quickly:

o **eRank** – Great for keyword volume and SEO tips. *(Free and paid versions)*
o **Everbee** – Chrome extension. *(Free for basic use (like keyword research), paid for full listing data)*
o **Alura** – Strong for tag insights and product performance trends. *(Paid)*
o **Marmalead** – Good for SEO and Etsy-specific market research. *(Paid)*

Check for Market Saturation vs Opportunity

How many listings exist for your idea? Lots of results might mean high demand—or high competition. Consider how you can niche down (like combining two themes) or present it with a fresh twist.

Think About Seasonality

Use Google Trends or tools like eRank's Trend Buzz to see if your product is seasonal (e.g., planners in December, teacher gifts in May). Timing matters!

Look Outside Etsy for Social Proof

Check Pinterest, TikTok, and Instagram—are people pinning or sharing products like yours? Are influencers talking about similar items? That's a great sign.

Bonus: Test Your Idea Fast

If you're still unsure about your idea, don't worry—you're not expected to publish a product today. But you can still test the waters a little:

• Create a simple preview in Canva—just a visual mockup that shows what your product would look like—and post it on Pinterest or Instagram to see if anyone engages.

• Share it with a few friends or in online spaces you trust, like a creative Facebook group or a Reddit thread. Ask what they think—what they'd expect it to include, or whether they'd use something like it.

- Pay attention to the reaction: Are people liking it? Saving it? Leaving comments or tagging others? Even small responses can tell you a lot.

Once we cover how to officially list products (coming up in Week 2), you'll already have a validated idea to move forward with—without starting from scratch.

The takeaway? Don't just look at what's popular—look at what's working and where you can bring your unique spin. That's your sweet spot.

You don't need to analyze forever. Give yourself about 20–30 minutes to explore. The goal isn't to become a market research expert—it's to spot demand and build confidence in your direction.

STEP 2: LET AI HELP WITH THE CONTENT

Let's say you choose a "Self-Care Checklist for Moms". Try a prompt like:

> *ACT AS A FRIENDLY WELLNESS COACH. CREATE A SIMPLE 10-POINT SELF-CARE CHECKLIST FOR BUSY MOMS. MAKE IT KIND AND ENCOURAGING.*

Or maybe you picked a gratitude journal page:

> *WRITE A ONE-PAGE JOURNALING PROMPT THAT INCLUDES A SPOT FOR NOTES, A POSITIVE*

Use the parts you like. Change anything that doesn't sound like you. This is your product.

You can even stack prompts: ask for a quote, then ask it to reword that quote in your own tone. Ask it for ideas to decorate your product. The more you play, the more ideas you'll get.

Note: If you're using Canva to design this product, it's important to understand how licensing works. You can sell products that use **free elements** from Canva—even as downloadable files like PDFs—as long as you're not violating their general use policies. However, **Canva Pro elements are different**:

- You cannot sell a downloadable file (like a planner PDF or wall art print) that includes Pro elements—even if you've customized them. The creators of those assets don't get credited or compensated when the file is sold this way.
- You can legally share your Canva product as a template link (using Canva's "share a copy" or contributor options). In this case, the end user will open the file in their own Canva account, and the original Pro asset creators will be paid properly when it's loaded.

But here's the catch: once you share that link with a customer, they can pass it along to others—and you have no control over how widely it's used.

To play it safe:

- Use only free Canva elements if you're planning to sell a digital download.

- If you're using Pro elements, offer it as a Canva template, and clearly state in your listing that the buyer will need a Canva account to use it.

Always double-check Canva's licensing policies (linked in the Bonus section) and keep your customers informed in your product description.

STEP 3: MAKE IT LOOK GOOD IN CANVA

Head to canva.com and choose a standard US Letter template (8.5 x 11 inches). Search for a layout that fits your product—like "checklist" or "planner"—and drop in your content.

Keep it clean and easy to read. Use simple fonts, add a little color, maybe toss in a few icons if you want. If you're not sure what looks good, start with a free template and tweak from there.

Pro Tip: Use the "Elements" tab in Canva to add shapes, icons or lines. These little touches can make your product feel more polished without much extra effort.

Important: Canva Pro assets shouldn't be used in downloadable items unless you have full rights through their terms. When in doubt—stick to free elements or modify templates significantly. We'll go over more Canva licensing details in the Bonus Materials.

When you're done, download your design as a high-quality PDF. Make sure you select "Best for printing" to get sharp results.

STEP 4: SAVE YOUR WORK

Create a folder on your computer (or Google Drive) just for your digital products. Save your Canva design and your final PDF there.

Pro Tip: Start a simple doc or spreadsheet where you track your product name, what it is, and a short description. You'll use this when it's time to upload to your store.

STEP 5: CREATE A MOCKUP (OPTIONAL BUT SMART)

If you want your product to stand out on Etsy or Gumroad, having a nice preview image helps a lot. You can use Canva again and search for "mockup" templates, or upload your PDF into a styled image.

Look for terms like "frame mockups," "desk flatlays," or "clipboard templates" to place your design in a real-world setting. But be mindful—don't use mockup templates that feature people in ways that could be offensive, sensitive, or imply things your product doesn't support. And again, always follow Canva's acceptable use policy.

Want your product image to look crisp? Canva recommends keeping thumbnail images around 600×800px when placing them on your website or Etsy listing. This helps protect the use of Canva's design assets and keeps file sizes manageable. You can still design and download your file in 'Best for printing' mode for physical products or print-on-demand—but if you're sharing a preview on your store page, keep it small and optimized.

Pro tip: Many print-on-demand platforms (like Printify or Gelato) offer their own built-in mockup builders. These tools automatically create styled product previews for your mugs, t-shirts, posters and more. It's a great alternative if you're designing something meant for physical sale!

WHAT YOU'VE LEARNED TODAY

Well done—you didn't just think about making a product today, you actually made one. That's a big deal. Maybe it's not perfect (and it doesn't need to be), but it's real. You figured out what kind of product to start with, tested your idea a bit, used AI to help shape the content, and brought it to life in Canva. You even took the extra step to make it look good with a mockup, if you had the time.

You've now got something that didn't exist yesterday—and that's the kind of progress that adds up fast.

DAY 3: CREATING DIGITAL PRODUCTS CHECKLIST

☐ Brainstorm 3 product types that align with your skills or interests

☐ Validate product demand using Etsy, Pinterest, and optional research tools like Everbee or eRank

☐ Choose one product idea to pursue today

☐ Write a short "elevator pitch" for your product idea

☐ Use ChatGPT (or Gemini / Claude) to help you outline or draft your content

☐ Design your product in Canva (using free or licensed assets)

☐ Export it as a high-quality PDF and save it to your digital product folder

☐ (Optional) Create a styled mockup preview in Canva

☐ Track your product and progress in a doc, sheet, or planner

You just made your first real product. That's not small—it's a major milestone. If you've got energy, keep going and make one more! But if not, give yourself credit: you've taken the leap from planning to doing. That's what this book is all about.

DAY 4: MIDJOURNEY & DALL·E FOR PRODUCT VISUALS

Welcome to Day 4! If you've ever said "I can't draw" or "I'm not a designer," this one's for you. Today is all about creating powerful product visuals—even if you've never designed a thing before. You'll learn how to use AI tools to make eye-catching images that work for print-on-demand products, social posts, or online listings.

Don't stress—this isn't a deep dive into complicated design software. We're keeping it simple and focused on results.

WHAT YOU'LL LEARN TODAY:

- The difference between DALL·E and Midjourney (and which to use for what)
- How to write visual prompts that get results
- How to use the art you create for products, mockups, or even social content

Let's get into it.

STEP 1: CHOOSE YOUR TOOL

Let's start by picking the right tool—one that matches how comfortable you are with trying something new.

If you're just starting out and want the easiest path, go with **DALL·E**. It's built right into ChatGPT Pro and doesn't need any extra steps. You just type what you want, and the image shows up. Quick and clean.

Midjourney creates more artistic and stylized images and lives on Discord. It requires a bit more setup but offers incredibly high-quality results. Use it if you're feeling a bit adventurous.

Here's how to get rolling:

To use DALL·E inside ChatGPT:

- Open ChatGPT Pro
- Start a new chat
- Type your visual request like you would ask any question

To use Midjourney:

1. If you don't have Discord yet, sign up at discord.com

2. Head to midjourney.com

3. Click "Sign Up" (or "Sign In" if you already have an account)

4. Accept the invitation to their server

5. Once you're in, find a channel labeled something like #newbies

6. Type /imagine followed by your image idea (you don't need to include the word "prompt"—just describe your idea)

Here are a few other tools you might want to explore if you're curious about alternatives:

- o **Leonardo.AI** – Offers sharp, highly customizable results. *Free to try with limitations.*
- o **Bing Image Creator** – Powered by DALL·E 3 *Fast and free, very beginner-friendly.*
- o **NightCafe** – Great if you want to try out artistic filters or stylized effects. *Offers a mix of free and paid options.*
- o **Craiyon** (formerly DALL·E Mini) *Totally free, quirky, and super basic.*

If you're curious, give them a shot as part of your practice. Some people find their favorite by experimenting a little. But in this guide, we'll focus on DALL·E and Midjourney because they hit the sweet spot of accessibility and image quality.

Just pick one and try it out. You're not committing to anything permanent—you're just exploring tools that can help bring your ideas to life.

STEP 2: CRAFTING A VISUAL PROMPT

Writing prompts for image generators is a bit different from chatting with tools like ChatGPT. Instead of asking a question, you're painting a picture with words—like describing a scene to a friend who's about to draw it for you. The clearer you are, the better the result.

Use this structure:

[Subject] + [Style] + [Mood or Detail] + [Background or Setting]

Examples:

> *A RETRO-STYLE COFFEE MUG DESIGN WITH THE WORDS 'MOM FUEL', BRIGHT COLORS, MINIMALIST ILLUSTRATION*

> *CUTE CARTOON CAT HOLDING A CUP OF TEA, WATERCOLOR EFFECT, WHITE BACKGROUND*

> *ELEGANT FLORAL PATTERN, SEAMLESS DESIGN, PASTEL TONES, FOR JOURNAL COVERS*

When creating visuals for products, try including phrases like "t-shirt graphic", "poster", or "printable art" to help the AI generate something that fits your end goal.

Want to test this? Try this in DALL·E:

> *CREATE A WATERCOLOR-STYLE ILLUSTRATION OF A COZY TEA MUG SURROUNDED BY FLOWERS.*

> *WHITE BACKGROUND. SUITABLE FOR A PRINTABLE ART PIECE.*

Or in Midjourney:

> */IMAGINE KAWAII-STYLE CARTOON BUNNY HOLDING A BALLOON, MINIMAL LINE ART, CLEAN WHITE BACKGROUND --V 6*

Be patient—sometimes you'll need a few tries to get something just right. You'll get better with every prompt.

Quick Note on Originality and Accidental Plagiarism

If you're planning to sell your AI-generated image, it's worth doing a quick gut check to make sure it doesn't look too much like something that already exists. While these tools aren't copying anything directly, sometimes the results can end up surprisingly similar to popular artwork or stock images.

You can use reverse image tools to check—just to be safe. They're not perfect (especially with AI images), but they're still useful:

o **TinEye** is good if you want to see whether an image or something super close to it already lives online.
o **Google Lens** lets you snap or upload an image and see what it finds visually similar across the web.
o **Bing Visual Search** is another option to try for cross-checking.

Again, this isn't an exact science—AI art is new territory—but if the design feels too familiar, don't ignore that feeling. Try adjusting the colors, style, or layout and run it again. When you're selling digital products, it's always better to be original than to take chances with something that could raise eyebrows (or worse).

STEP 3: DOWNLOAD AND CLEAN UP YOUR IMAGE

Once your image is ready, download it.

- In DALL·E (ChatGPT), click on the image, then download.
- In Midjourney, right-click the image and choose "Save image as".

If needed, you can use Canva or remove.bg to remove the background, add text, or layer your design into a product mockup.

Pro tip: Create a folder on your computer just for your AI-generated images and mockups. Organize by project or product type.

STEP 4: ADD YOUR DESIGN TO A PRODUCT

Now that you've got your image, try dropping it onto something real—like a mug or a tote bag—just to see how it looks. Canva works great for this, or you can use the mockup tools inside Printify or Printful if that's where you're headed.

Play with the size and placement a bit. Maybe the design looks better off-center, or maybe it pops more on a darker background. There's no exact formula—just test things until something clicks. When you've got a version you like, save it. You'll need those mockups later when it's time to show off your product.

Also, do yourself a favor and make a folder to keep all this stuff in one place. Call it something like "AI Designs" or "Mockups" so you don't lose track of everything. (Yes, this is one of those boring-sounding tips that actually helps a ton.)

One more thing: If your image doesn't look quite right the first time, no worries. That's totally normal. Just go back, tweak the prompt a little—change the color, the mood, the wording. Sometimes one small change makes all the difference.

Think of this as playing with a new creative toy—have fun and let your ideas evolve as you go.

Want your image to pop? Export at high resolution:

In Canva, choose "Best for Printing" when downloading a .pdf file

In Printify, use their built-in mockup tools

Reminder: Canva Pro elements cannot be sold as digital downloads unless heavily customized or shared as a Canva template link. See Canva's licensing terms for details (linked in the Bonus section).

Also, mockups can be created directly on platforms like Printify, which saves time and gives you more accurate previews.

IMPORTANT NOTE ON ETHICS AND QUALITY

Before you upload that image… perform a quick reality check

It's easy to get excited when your AI image turns out looking pretty great—but before you hit download and call it done, take a good look. Even when an image seems finished, little things can be off. You might spot some weird fingers, a strange blur in the corner, or text that just doesn't look right. These little hiccups are called "AI artifacts," and while they're common, they can make your product feel a bit off if left untouched.

Give your image a once-over and ask:

- Do the lines look clean and intentional?

- Are any details missing, distorted, or oddly placed?

- Does everything feel balanced and easy to understand at a glance?

If something feels off, don't toss the whole thing—just tweak it. You can either go back and adjust your prompt (sometimes just adding one extra detail helps), or do some quick clean-up work with editing tools:

o **Photopea** is a great free option that feels like Photoshop but runs in your browser.

o **Photoshop** is perfect if you already use it and want more control.

o **Canva** is great for smaller tweaks—like cropping, moving layers, or adjusting layout.

Ethically speaking, it's important to treat AI like a creative assistant, not a one-click shortcut. When you tweak and improve what it gives you, your product becomes more original, more polished, and way more sellable.

PRACTICE: YOUR TURN

Now it's your turn. Open DALL·E or Midjourney and try making 1–2 product-ready visuals based on a niche you're excited about. Here are a few ideas:

- A coffee mug design with a motivational quote
- A minimalist animal line drawing for a t-shirt
- A cozy watercolor tea illustration for wall art
- A floral pattern for a journal cover

Use Canva or Photopea to place your image into a product mockup, save both the image and the mockup and store your editable files, too—you'll want to tweak or reuse them later. You now have real visuals you could list tomorrow.

You don't have to share it with the world yet—this is just for you. But if you can create one strong image today, that's a win.

WHAT YOU'VE LEARNED TODAY

- Picked a visual AI tool (DALL·E or Midjourney)
- Learned how to write effective image prompts
- Practiced fixing visual issues and cleaning up artwork
- Created and saved your own product visuals
- Placed your images into mockups, ready for your store

That's a full creative day—well done!

DAY 4: CREATE A DESIGN USING AI CHECKLIST

☐ Choose your image tool (DALL·E or Midjourney) and set up your account (unless done on Day 1)

☐ Write 2–3 image prompts using the structure: subject + style + mood + setting

☐ Generate and download at least one product-ready image

☐ Check the image for visual flaws or AI artifacts

☐ Fix any issues using Canva, Photopea, or Photoshop

☐ Place your final image into a product mockup

☐ Save your editable version + the final version

☐ Organize your files in folders by product type or theme

☐ Optional: Try the same prompt with a small tweak to see how it changes

DAY 5: AI VIDEO CREATION

Welcome to Day 5! Today we're getting into something a little more dynamic—video. And before you panic, no, you don't need a fancy camera, a microphone setup, or editing experience. All you really need is curiosity and a few easy-to-use tools. Thanks to AI, making short, scroll-stopping videos is way more doable than it used to be. Whether you want to promote your products or just start showing up online more confidently, today's the day to give it a shot.

You might've noticed we didn't throw video tools at you back on Day 1—and that was on purpose. Not everyone is ready to dive into video right away. If today feels like too much, that's totally fine. Bookmark it and come back later. But if you're ready? This might be the push you didn't know you needed.

WHY EVEN BOTHER WITH VIDEO?

Here's the deal: video content grabs attention—fast. A quick 15 to 30-second clip can stop someone mid-scroll way more often than a static post. It's especially powerful on platforms like Instagram, TikTok, and Pinterest, where movement = engagement.

You don't have to go full influencer mode. Just a simple video can:

- Show what your product actually looks like in use
- Build a bit of trust and familiarity with your audience

• Help your content surface more in search and algorithm feeds

Whether you use your videos for social posts, product listings, or even quick ads, having a couple under your belt is a serious bonus—and surprisingly easy once you try it.

TOOLS TO TRY (FREE & PAID)

Here are some tools that make video creation simple:

o **Pictory** – Great for beginners. Turn a short script into a video with AI-selected visuals and music. *(Free trial available)*
o **InVideo** – Choose templates, type your message, and let it build a full video. *(Free/paid)*
o **Lumen5** – Turn text into animated scenes. *(Free limited version)*
o **Canva Video** – This is not AI-powered but offers beautiful pre-made templates with drag-and-drop editing. Great for clean, no-fuss videos. *(Free)*
o **Synthesia** or **HeyGen** – Create AI avatar-style videos with voiceovers. More advanced, great for certain niches. *(Paid)*

We're focusing on **Pictory** and **Canva Video** because they strike a good balance of ease and power. Pictory uses AI to help assemble your video, while Canva gives you full control in a very intuitive way.

STEP-BY-STEP: WRITE A NATURAL-SOUNDING PROMO SCRIPT

Let's say you've created a product like a self-care journal. You want to explain what it is and why someone would love it—in about 2–4 sentences. That's it.

Example:

> *FEELING STRESSED? THIS PRINTABLE SELF-CARE JOURNAL GIVES YOU 5 MINUTES OF PEACE AND CLARITY EVERY DAY. THOUGHTFULLY DESIGNED FOR BUSY MOMS. DOWNLOAD YOURS NOW ON ETSY.*

Keep it short, natural, and kind. You're just talking to another person, not reading a corporate pitch.

If you're stuck, you can ask ChatGPT to suggest a few starting points:

> *CAN YOU GIVE ME 3 PROMOTIONAL MESSAGE IDEAS FOR A PRINTABLE GRATITUDE JOURNAL?"*

But don't copy and paste the AI's text. Rewrite it in your own tone. People know when something's been copy-pasted from a bot—and that's when trust drops. Perfectly imperfect language that sounds like you will always connect better.

STEP-BY-STEP: BUILD THE VIDEO

With Pictory:

1. Paste your short script into the dashboard

2. Let it pick visuals (you can swap any you don't like)

3. Choose background music

4. Preview, adjust text timing, and export

With Canva Video:

1. Start a new video project using a "Reel" or "TikTok" template

2. Add your script one sentence per scene

3. Drop in product mockups, photos, or AI images you've made

4. Animate the text or background (optional)

5. Export when you're happy with it

Try to keep each video between 15–30 seconds. Short, clear, and visually appealing always wins.

Start with these 3 ad-style prompts:

1. For a mug: "Mom Fuel in a Cup" – design a script that's fun, relatable, and energetic

2. For a wall art print: "Pause. Breathe. Begin Again". – script something calming and motivational

3. For a sticker pack: "Made for Chaos Coordinators" – something bold and playful

Create 2–3 different videos using these prompts. Try switching:

- The product focus
- The tone (cheerful vs. sincere vs. quirky)
- The tool (try one in Canva, another in Pictory)

Even if you never publish them, you'll be surprised how much easier it gets after a couple tries.

WHAT YOU'VE LEARNED TODAY

- A human-style script that connects without sounding robotic
- Your first promo videos, done in a few clicks
- More confidence in how to use visuals and tone to sell without feeling salesy

You've got something powerful in your pocket now. Tomorrow, we'll make your online presence easier by having ChatGPT help with social media planning. See you then!

DAY 5: MAKE A SHORT VIDEO CHECKLIST

☐ Write a short, natural-sounding product script

☐ Use Canva or Pictory to create a short promo video

☐ Include trending audio or captions if needed

☐ Test at least one video with different visuals or tones

☐ Export and save your video

☐ Optional: Create 1–2 variations using different tools, styles, or messages

DAY 6: SOCIAL MEDIA CONTENT WITH CHATGPT

Welcome to Day 6! You've got a few products under your belt now—and maybe even a video or two. Today, we're going to talk about something that can either fuel your momentum or quietly stall it: showing up on social media.

Now don't worry—this isn't about turning you into an influencer. You don't need to dance on camera or post five times a day. What you do need is a way to start putting your work out there in a way that feels comfortable and consistent.

The good news? Tools like ChatGPT (or Gemini, or Claude—whichever you prefer) can help take a lot of the stress out of it. You don't have to sit around wondering what to say or how to say it. Think of it like having a helpful brainstorming buddy that throws out ideas when you're stuck—not someone writing everything for you, but someone to get the wheels turning.

WHY THIS MATTERS

Think of social media like waving to someone from across the street. You're not yelling, "Buy this now!"—you're just showing up, being seen, and letting people get familiar with you. That simple presence builds trust, even if they're not ready to buy yet.

And when they are ready? You won't be a stranger.

Still, let's be honest. Sitting down and thinking, What do I post today? every single day can get exhausting fast. That's where tools like ChatGPT come in handy—not as your copywriter, but as a sounding board. It's like having a friend you can bounce ideas off when your brain feels empty.

You still get to sound like you. You still decide what goes out. But now you're not starting from a blank screen.

STEP 1: PICK A PLATFORM (OR TWO)

You don't need to be everywhere. Pick just one or two places where you'll start showing up—and stick with them for now. Think about your comfort level and where your audience might naturally be.

o **Instagram** is great if you enjoy visuals, sharing your creative process, or making short videos.

o **Pinterest** works well if you want your content to be searchable and evergreen—especially for planners, checklists, or aesthetic designs.

o **TikTok** is your go-to for quick, relatable content with personality. (And yes, you can reuse what you made on Day 5!)

o **Facebook** or **Threads** is more about storytelling and creating conversations—ideal for those who like writing or engaging in communities.

Still not sure where to start? Go with the platform you already use the most. It's easier to be consistent when it feels familiar.

STEP 2: USE CHATGPT (OR GEMINI / CLAUDE) TO BRAINSTORM POST IDEAS

Coming up with daily content can feel like a full-time job. The good news? You don't have to start from scratch.

Fire up ChatGPT and try this kind of prompt:

CAN YOU GIVE ME 10 POST IDEAS FOR A NEW INSTAGRAM PAGE THAT FEATURES PRINTABLE SELF-CARE TOOLS FOR MOMS? I WANT A MIX OF HELPFUL, FUN, AND PERSONAL IDEAS

Once you have a list, you can follow up with:

CAN YOU ORGANIZE THOSE INTO A SIMPLE 5-DAY CONTENT CALENDAR WITH CAPTION STARTERS?

You'll probably want to rewrite a few things to sound more like you—but it's much easier to edit than to stare at a blank screen.

STEP 3: ADJUST IT TO SOUND LIKE YOU

Use the ideas from ChatGPT as a draft. Rewrite any captions that sound too formal, too "salesy", or too generic. Here's an example:

Too robotic:

> *DOWNLOAD THIS CHECKLIST TODAY TO OPTIMIZE YOUR WELLNESS HABITS*

More human:

> *HONESTLY, THIS SELF-CARE CHECKLIST IS THE ONLY REASON I REMEMBER TO DRINK WATER AND PUT MY PHONE DOWN BEFORE BED. IT'S NOT FANCY—BUT IT WORKS*

That's the kind of tone that sticks. Real. Relatable. A little imperfect.

STEP 4: ADD SOME VARIETY

If you're not sure what to post, don't worry—there's no need to reinvent the wheel every time. Start with a few simple content types and rotate through them as needed. For example:

- Snap a behind-the-scenes photo: your workspace, a messy sketchpad, or your Canva screen mid-project
- Share a mockup or preview of a product you're working on
- Offer a quick "Did you know?" tip related to your niche
- Post a short personal win, lesson learned, or story about your process
- Add a quote from a customer—or use a placeholder until you have real ones

- Ask a fun question or run a casual poll (people love to weigh in!)

Now let's talk about how to actually get those posts out without burning out.

You may have heard of tools like **Later** or **Buffer**—but what do they actually do?

These tools help you plan, schedule, and post your content automatically across platforms like Instagram, Facebook, Pinterest, and more. Instead of logging in every day, you can batch your content once a week, set it, and forget it.

Later – Offers a visual content calendar so you can drag and drop your posts where you want them. Offers a 14-day free trial with plans starting at $16.67/month billed annually or $25/month billed monthly. You'll connect your social media account (yes, you give it permission), and 'Later' handles the posting for you.

Buffer – Another popular option that's clean and easy to use. It lets you write captions, upload images or videos, and pick times for posting. It also requires connecting your account, and it's safe and widely trusted. Has a free plan with limited features. Paid plans start at $5/month per channel (or $60/year).

Both platforms are safe to use—but be mindful of what permissions you grant. Always connect through secure login (not password sharing), and check your settings so you're only giving access to the pages or accounts you need.

That said, neither Buffer nor Later includes a built-in music library. And because they're third-party tools, they can't access the licensed audio catalog from platforms like Instagram or TikTok. So, if you want music in your post or Reel, you'll need to add it beforehand.

Tools like **CapCut** (free and beginner-friendly) or **InShot** (another easy-to-use app with free + paid features) are perfect for adding audio, trimming video, or creating short, snappy clips. You can add trending songs, voiceovers, or sound effects—then export and upload your video to Instagram or TikTok with the audio already included.

If scheduling tools feel like too much right now, you've got other options. Instagram, for example, lets you schedule posts right inside the app. You can plan your week's content all at once, hit 'schedule', and be done—no extra tools needed.

Whatever method you choose, remember: don't "post it and ghost it." Social media is meant to be social. If people comment, react, or ask questions, try to respond. It builds trust and shows you're a real person behind the screen, not just another sales account.

And since your store likely isn't live yet, here's the real purpose of these early posts: warming up your audience. You're not pushing for sales—you're inviting people into the journey. Show them what you're working on, tease new products, and even ask for their thoughts. Questions like:

- "Which design do you prefer—A or B?"

- "What would you expect to pay for something like this?"
- "If you could only pick two: great price, standout design, or super quality?"

You're not selling yet. You're building curiosity, starting conversations, and collecting valuable feedback so when your shop does go live, it doesn't feel like a cold start.

PRACTICE: YOUR TURN (BUILD A 5-DAY POST PLAN)

Open ChatGPT and work on this simple task:

> *HELP ME CREATE A 5-DAY INSTAGRAM CONTENT PLAN FOR PROMOTING A PRINTABLE MUG DESIGN FOR MOMS.*

Once you have that, tweak the captions and images, and get them ready to post.

Then try again for a different product:

> *NOW MAKE A PLAN FOR PROMOTING A MOTIVATIONAL WALL ART DOWNLOAD.*

Once you get the hang of it, you'll never have to stare at a blinking cursor again, and the more you practice this, the more natural content creation will feel.

WHAT YOU'VE LEARNED TODAY

You've done a lot today. You came up with real post ideas, mapped out a content plan you can actually stick with, and started shaping those AI-generated blurbs into something that sounds like you. That's not just checking boxes—that's laying the groundwork for showing up online in a way that feels real. And honestly, that's what people connect with.

Tomorrow, we'll ease into the finish line of Week 1 by putting together a few simple but high-impact products—think lighthearted quizzes, easy-to-use templates, and small bonus items that can make your shop feel more personal and generous. These are quick to create, but they can really make your listings stand out. You'll see what I mean.

DAY 6: START POSTING ON SOCIALS CHECKLIST

☐ Pick 1–2 social platforms to focus on

☐ Draft 3–5 posts using your product visuals or mockups

☐ Use ChatGPT to brainstorm new caption ideas

☐ Schedule your posts with Instagram, Later, or Buffer

☐ Reply to at least 3 people in your niche or community

☐ Ask 1–2 audience-building questions (polls, "this or that," etc.)

☐ Save your captions and ideas in a social media folder or doc

Tomorrow, we'll shift gears and work on "easy win" digital products—like printable quizzes, thoughtful templates, and fun little extras your audience will love.

DAY 7: EASY WINS – QUIZZES, TEMPLATES, AND BONUSES

Here we are—Day 7! If you've stuck with this all week, you've already accomplished more than most people do when they say they want to "start something." You've set up your tools, made your first product, explored visuals and video, and even dipped into social media. That's a full plate—and you've handled it.

Today is about lightening things up a bit with digital products that are quick to create but still useful and memorable. Think: personality quizzes, simple templates, or bonus goodies like a printable sticker sheet. They may not take long to build, but they can add a surprising amount of value to your shop—and a lot of charm too.

This is your chance to add a little personality, give your buyers a helpful extra, and remind yourself that not every product has to be a massive project to be meaningful.

WHY THESE PRODUCTS WORK

Here's why they're worth your time:

- **Quizzes** make people feel seen. They're lighthearted, personal, and easy to share.
- **Templates** save buyers the effort of starting from scratch. Everyone loves a plug-and-play solution.

- **Bonuses** (like printable stickers or maze pages) add a thoughtful human touch to your product—and show you care about the person behind the purchase.

Let's dive into a few examples.

1. Quizzes That Entertain or Inform

Use ChatGPT (or Gemini / Claude) to brainstorm and shape a quiz your audience would enjoy. These could be silly, personality-based, or genuinely helpful.

Try this:

> *HELP ME CREATE A 5-QUESTION PERSONALITY QUIZ FOR MOMS: "WHAT TYPE OF MORNING MOM ARE YOU?" INCLUDE 4 RESULT TYPES WITH A SHORT DESCRIPTION FOR EACH.*

You can drop this into a Canva template and export as a printable PDF, or if you prefer an interactive version, use Google Forms or Typeform.

2. Templates That Make Life Easier

Think planners, trackers, or checklists. You can create these using a blank Canva file—just keep it neat, practical, and visually simple.

Some starter ideas:

- A "reset routine" checklist
- A weekly social media post planner

- A daily gratitude tracker

Prompt idea for ChatGPT:

> *I'M MAKING A WEEKLY PLANNER FOR PARENTS. WHAT ARE 10 THINGS THEY MIGHT WANT TO KEEP TRACK OF?*

Important: If you use Canva templates, make sure to modify them enough so that they are clearly your own. Change layout, colors, fonts, elements—whatever it takes to make the final design original. Canva's license doesn't allow you to sell unedited templates, and one bad review online can do real damage. Protect the brand you're building.

3. Add-On Bonuses: Little Extras That Delight

You don't need to give away your best product to stand out. Instead, think of a small bonus that adds heart to your work. For example:

- A printable sticker page with affirmations or cute designs
- A coloring mini-poster with your product's theme
- A maze for a customer's child, tied to the product they bought

This kind of thoughtful detail turns a standard download into a memorable experience. It also subtly builds trust—people remember when you go the extra step.

Prompt idea:

> *CREATE A BLACK-AND-WHITE PRINTABLE MAZE FOR KIDS WITH A SIMPLE GARDEN THEME. MAKE IT EASY FOR AGES 5–8.*

Customize it. Brand it. Make it feel like it came from you, not a robot.

PRACTICE: YOUR TURN. MAKE ONE OF EACH

Before you wrap today, see if you can create:

- One short quiz (title, questions, results)
- One simple planner or template
- One thoughtful extra (sticker page, mini activity, or thank-you note)

You don't need to publish these yet—just treat them as drafts and get them ready to use later, either in your store or as free bonuses.

Bonus Tip: Bundle it

When you have a few of these small products, think about grouping them together:

- A planner, tracker, and checklist = Productivity Starter Kit
- A quiz and a journal page = Self-Discovery Pack

Bundles increase the perceived value without increasing your effort. And when you offer a little extra? People remember.

- Discovered fast, low-effort product types people actually want
- Used AI to generate ideas, questions, layouts, and line art
- Designed three digital products you can list or expand later

DAY 7: PLAN BONUSES AND ADD-ONS CHECKLIST

☐ Brainstorm 2–3 themed bonus ideas

☐ Use ChatGPT to help write quiz questions and outcomes

☐ Design one simple add-on (like a printable or sticker sheet)

☐ Ensure your design is original—customize fonts, colors, layout

☐ Make sure your bonus complements the main product

☐ Save and store it for your product listing

☐ Optional: Combine a few items into a bundle idea you could sell or offer as a gift

WEEK 1 RECAP: WHAT YOU'VE BUILT SO FAR

Take a deep breath—you've just wrapped up an incredibly productive first week. Whether you've been breezing through or taking it one task at a time, you're now standing on a foundation stronger than most beginners ever build.

Here's what you've accomplished:

- **Installed and set up your core toolkit** — you signed up for essential platforms like ChatGPT, Canva, and either Midjourney or DALL·E. You might've also installed handy browser extensions and created accounts for platforms like Notion or Google Docs. If you didn't get to those yet, no worries—we'll dig deeper into how and when to use them in Week 2. That wasn't a miss; it was intentional. I didn't want to throw too much at you on Day 1.

- **Learned how to work with your first 3 tools** — you've now had hands-on experience using ChatGPT for brainstorming, Canva for product design and mockups, and DALL·E or Midjourney for visuals. You've not only explored how to use them—you've used them with purpose.

- **Created your first product** — whether it was a printable, a planner, a journal prompt, or a checklist, you've taken something from idea to execution. It's no longer just a concept—it's a digital product with real potential.

- **Practiced visual design** — you created AI-generated artwork, cleaned it up, and mocked it into a real product format. You also learned to spot and correct AI mistakes (hello, six-fingered hands and floating teacups).

- **Built a short promotional video** — you drafted your first script, matched it with visuals and music, and produced a mini video ad using either Pictory or Canva Video. Not bad for a week's work!

- **Started warming up your audience** — even without a store, you brainstormed social content, created polls and posts, and learned how to speak to your future customers like a real person—not a pushy salesperson.

- **Added some personal flair** — you made or planned thoughtful extras like printable stickers, maze pages, or quiz-based downloads. Whether you include them as bonuses or bundle them into small offers, you've now got more to offer than just a single product.

WHAT'S COMING IN WEEK 2

Week 2 is about turning your creativity into a real, sellable offer. That means:

- Setting up your online store (Etsy, Gumroad, or another platform)

- Creating listings that connect with the right audience

- Choosing the right pricing strategy so your product feels worth it—without scaring off potential buyers

- Making sure your designs are actually ready to deliver

- Talking about customer experience, from the very first click to post-purchase follow-up

You're about to step into a new role: **creator AND seller**. But don't worry—we're doing it together. By the end of Week 2, you'll have a real storefront, at least one listing ready to go, and the clarity to keep building from there.

No fluff. No guesswork. Just simple, clear, repeatable steps you can grow with.

Let's make it happen.

WEEK 2:

BUILDING ASSETS

DAY 8: CHOOSE YOUR SELLING PLATFORM AND SET UP YOUR STORE

You've made it through the first week—and that's no small thing. You've created real products, played with visuals, even dipped your toes into social media and video. That's a solid foundation. Now it's time to shift gears.

This week, we're moving from creating to selling. It's not just about having digital products—it's about getting them in front of people who want to buy them.

So let's kick things off with a key question: Where are you actually going to sell your stuff?

There's no one-size-fits-all answer. But in the next few pages, we'll break down the most popular platforms in plain English— what each one offers, what to look out for, and how much effort it takes to get started.

ETSY

If you're planning to sell things like printables, planners, digital journals, or cute stickers, Etsy is a great place to start.

People love Etsy because it already brings in shoppers who are actively searching for these kinds of products. You don't have to worry about setting up your own website or finding ways to accept payments—Etsy handles all of that for you.

You'll need about $15–$20 to get going. There's a $15 one-time verification fee, plus a small $0.20 charge every time you list a product (which renews every 3 months).

That said, Etsy isn't a secret anymore. There are a lot of sellers, so standing out takes a bit of effort. And yes, Etsy does take a small cut from each sale (around 6.5%, plus payment processing fees).

So why are we starting here? Because it's beginner-friendly. You don't need a big following or fancy tools to launch. If you've got a product and a few mockups, you're good to go.

GUMROAD

Gumroad is a solid choice if you're looking to sell straightforward digital products like PDF guides, art prints, toolkits, or even offer "pay what you want" downloads.

It's especially handy if you already have an audience—say, through social media, a blog, or an email list—since Gumroad doesn't have a built-in marketplace to bring in shoppers. You'll be directing traffic to your products yourself.

Getting started is free. For sales you bring in directly (like through your own links or profile), Gumroad takes a 10% cut plus a $0.50 fee per transaction . However, if a customer discovers your product through Gumroad's "Discover" marketplace, the fee jumps to 30% . That's why it really pays off to bring people in through your own links whenever you can. You'll keep more of each sale that way.

Getting your store up and running on Gumroad doesn't take much time, which makes it a good spot to test ideas or set up a clean, simple shop. Just keep in mind—because there's no big marketplace helping you out, it's on you to spread the word and get your products in front of the right people.

AMAZON (THREE PATHS)

Amazon's a huge platform with massive reach—but getting started there isn't quite as simple as it sounds. There are three main ways you can sell, and each has its own quirks.

1. Print-on-Demand with Printify

This setup lets you design something—like a mug or a tote bag—and have a print-on-demand service (such as Printify) handle the rest. When someone places an order on Amazon, Printify takes care of printing and shipping it.

The good news? You don't need to hold any inventory. The entire process is automated once everything is linked up.

But there's a catch: you'll need to either get approved for Amazon's **Merch on Demand** program (which can involve waiting), or create a regular seller account and connect Printify manually.

Fees and commission:

- Printify charges you per item to make and ship it.

- Amazon also takes a cut, called a referral fee.

- If you go with an **Individual Seller account**, there's no monthly subscription—just a $0.99 fee per item sold.

- If you're selling more consistently, you'll likely want a **Professional Seller account**, which costs $39.99/month. That unlocks features like bulk uploading, ads, and custom branding.

Oh—and one important heads-up: **you can't sell digital downloads on Amazon**. Want to sell eBooks? That's through Kindle Direct Publishing, which is a whole other ballgame we won't get into here.

2. Fulfilled by Amazon (FBA)

This one's for folks with physical inventory on hand. You send your products to Amazon's warehouses, and they handle shipping, returns, and customer support.

It's a great way to tap into Amazon's fast delivery and Prime perks—but it does require you to invest in inventory up front. You'll also need to cover storage and fulfillment fees, which can add up quickly.

3. Amazon Storefront (Affiliate or Brand)

If you already sell on Amazon or have affiliate products you want to showcase, you can set up a custom storefront.

You'll be able to highlight products in one place—even if they're not your own—but it's not ideal for newcomers. You can't just list Printify items unless those exact products already exist on Amazon.

Why We're Holding Off on Amazon (for Now)

Amazon is great when you've got momentum—but it's not the easiest place to start from scratch.

For one, **you can't sell digital printables there**. Only physical goods are allowed. Yes, you can publish eBooks—but that's through Kindle, and it's a whole different workflow.

Then there's the competition. Amazon is crowded, and most new listings don't get much love unless you're running ads or already have strong sales and reviews. You could spend a lot on ads and still be buried in the search results.

Print-on-demand is doable—but only for physical goods. And even then, you have to deal with setup steps, seller fees, approval delays, and tighter margins.

This book is about getting your shop off the ground **quickly and without a huge upfront investment**. Amazon just doesn't offer that kind of flexibility at the beginning. But once you're up and running and want to scale? By all means, come back to it later.

EBAY (OPTIONAL)

If you're already familiar with eBay or want to offer printable downloads or templates, it can work—but the setup is more manual, and traffic isn't always looking for digital items.

If you're already posting regularly and building a bit of a following, Instagram Shop can be a great way to turn those likes into actual sales. It lets your audience shop right from your feed—without needing to send them to another site (unless you want to).

Who's it for?

If you're already sharing photos, stories, or reels and starting to build a little community, this could be a good next step. Instagram Shop works best when you've got a consistent posting routine and a feed that reflects your brand's personality.

How to set it up:

You'll need to switch to a Business or Creator account, and then set up a product catalog using Meta Commerce Manager. If you're using Etsy or Shopify, you can connect your store to Instagram through built-in integrations—super handy.

How orders work:

If you direct people to Etsy or Shopify, those platforms (and tools like Printify or Printful) take care of order fulfilment.

If you let customers check out directly on Instagram, you'll either need to handle the shipping yourself or connect a system that does.

Fees and commission:

Instagram charges a 5% transaction fee for anything bought through their in-app checkout. If you're sending people off-platform (like to your Etsy shop), you'll still pay whatever fees those platforms charge—including shipping and fulfilment costs.

Heads-up:

It's easy to fall into the trap of trying to be everywhere at once. Instagram Shop is a great expansion move, but don't feel like you need to launch everything all at once. Focus on getting one platform running smoothly first—then layer this in when you're ready.

TIKTOK SHOP

If you've already started building a presence on TikTok, this might be your moment to turn those views into real sales. TikTok Shop lets people buy directly from your videos, livestreams, and profile—without ever leaving the app.

Who's it for?

If you're already sharing regularly on TikTok and getting some traction—likes, comments, or even just steady views—this might be a good fit. It's a solid option for anyone who feels comfortable in front of the camera and wants to turn that creative energy into sales.

Getting started:

You'll need a TikTok Business account, and then register through the TikTok Shop Seller Center. They'll ask for your ID or business paperwork, and once you're in, you can list your products manually or connect through platforms like Shopify, WooCommerce, or BigCommerce.

How orders work:

If you're using TikTok's native checkout, you'll either need to ship orders yourself or use a fulfillment tool that integrates through something like Shopify. TikTok doesn't link directly with Etsy or Gumroad, so those paths won't work for automated orders.

Fees and commission:

TikTok takes a small cut of each sale—usually somewhere between 2% and 5%. Sometimes they lower the rate during special promos for new sellers, so keep an eye out for that if you're just getting started.

If you're just getting started, you can absolutely come back to TikTok Shop later. But if you already have momentum on the platform? This could be a great way to build on it.

Can I sell directly on Printify?

Not really. Printify is a production platform—it fulfills orders but doesn't offer a public storefront. You'll need to connect it to Etsy, Shopify, or another marketplace.

STEP-BY-STEP: SET UP YOUR FIRST STORE

Let's walk through setting up your first store on Etsy—since that's the most beginner-friendly platform for new creators. Once your Etsy shop is up and running (or if you already have a loyal following), you can also choose to open an Instagram or TikTok Shop to expand your reach.

1. Create your account

Use a business email so you can keep store-related things separate.

2. Name your shop

Pick something that's short, easy to remember, and flexible enough to grow with you. Don't stress—it doesn't have to be perfect. If you feel stuck, you can use ChatGPT (or Gemini / Claude) to help brainstorm. Try asking:

> *GIVE ME 10 SHOP NAME IDEAS FOR A STORE THAT SELLS DIGITAL PLANNERS AND SELF-CARE PRINTABLES. KEEP THEM FUN AND CREATIVE.*

You can also ask it to help shape your mission statement or brand tone. Think of ChatGPT as your brainstorming buddy, not your final voice.

3. Upload a profile photo and banner

Use Canva to design a simple shop banner. Even if it's temporary, it should reflect your vibe.

4. Add a shop description

Tell people what they can expect from you: your tone, your mission, or who your products are for.

5. Connect your payout details

Etsy will ask for your bank account or PayPal so you can get paid. Totally normal.

6. Save your store link

Copy the URL and save it along with your login details—but do it safely. Avoid storing passwords in plain text (like in Notion or Google Docs). Instead, use a password manager.

Here are a few options:

o **KeePassXC**: A downloadable desktop app. Doesn't sync between devices automatically, but you can use it with KeePass Touch on mobile as a workaround. *(Free)*
o **Bitwarden**: A secure app and browser extension that syncs across devices. Easy to use and widely trusted. *(Freemium)*
o **LastPass**, **1Password**, or **Strongbox**: Other good options depending on your preferences and budget.

These tools help you stay organized, secure, and stress-free as your store grows.

HOW TO CONNECT ETSY WITH PRINTIFY

If you're using Printify for your physical products, it's smart to connect it to Etsy so fulfillment happens automatically.

1. Create your Printify account

Head to https://printify.com and sign up for free.

2. From the dashboard, click "Manage Stores"

This is where you'll connect your selling platforms.

3. Choose Etsy and click "Connect"

You'll be redirected to Etsy to log in and authorize Printify to manage orders and products.

4. Once connected, you can start creating products

Use Printify's design tool to add your art to mockups (mugs, shirts, wall art, etc.).

Once you create your first listing (we'll cover it tomorrow), your Etsy orders will automatically route to Printify, and they'll handle the printing and shipping for you. You just focus on creating and growing.

WHAT YOU'VE LEARNED TODAY

Today marked a big shift—you're no longer just planning, you're setting up shop for real. You explored the top platforms out there, from Etsy and Gumroad to Amazon, Instagram Shop, and TikTok Shop, and started to get a feel for what makes each one tick. You saw why Etsy tends to be the go-to for new sellers: it's easy to get started, doesn't require upfront inventory, and comes with a built-in audience already looking for what you're making.

You also went step-by-step through setting up your Etsy store—from choosing your shop name to uploading your banner and locking in your payout info. If you're planning to sell physical products, you learned how to connect your Etsy account to Printify so that orders can be fulfilled without you having to lift a finger.

Bottom line: your store is no longer just an idea floating in your head. It's up, it's real, and you're ready to make your first sale.

PRACTICE: YOUR TURN

This isn't the day to list your products. Just focus on:

- Picking your platform
- Creating your storefront
- Filling in your brand basics

Log your shop name, email, login info, and store link in a safe place.

You now have a home for your products. Tomorrow, we'll work on creating your very first listing the right way.

This is getting real—and you're doing great.

DAY 8: SET UP YOUR STORE CHECKLIST

☐ Choose your selling platform (Etsy, Gumroad, etc.)

☐ Create your store profile and name

☐ Write a short store bio/about section

☐ Upload your banner and profile image (Canva makes this easy)

☐ Connect payment methods securely

☐ Use a password manager to store login info

☐ Bookmark your store link for easy access

☐ Connect Etsy with Printify to automate fulfilment (if selling physical goods)

☐ Save your brand and login details in a secure place

DAY 9: CREATE AND PUBLISH YOUR FIRST PRODUCT LISTING

Your store's up and running—nice work! Now comes the exciting part: putting your first product out into the world. This step is more than just uploading a file—it's your chance to introduce your brand, your style, and your vibe to potential customers.

You've already done the hard part—making the thing. Now, you'll package it up in a way that helps people instantly understand what it is, who it's for, and why it's worth checking out.

STEP 1: PICKING YOUR FIRST PRODUCT

If you've got a few creations sitting in your folder, you might be asking yourself, "Which one should I go with first?" Don't overthink it. Choose the one that feels solid—the one you'd be most comfortable showing a stranger.

A few gut-check questions can help:

- Is the file ready to go (PDF, PNG, JPG, or maybe a ZIP)?
- Did you name it something clear and clean (instead of "final_version_final_EDITED_use_this_one")?
- Do you feel good putting your name next to it?

It doesn't have to be perfect—it just has to be real. One good listing is more than most people ever get to. You're doing it.

STEP 2: PRICE IT

Let's talk numbers—but keep it simple. Your first price tag isn't carved in stone. Think of it as a starting point, not a forever commitment.

If you're selling a quick printable—something like a one-page checklist or a simple tracker—most listings land somewhere between **$1.99** and **$5.99**. If it's a planner, a bundle, or anything that includes multiple pages or extra value, you're looking at more like **$6.99** to **$14.99**.

Not sure where you fall? Take five minutes to browse similar listings on Etsy or Gumroad. What are others charging for something close to yours? Use that as a loose guide, but don't feel like you have to match the lowest price out there. You made something thoughtful—don't undervalue it.

And remember: you can always tweak your price later if needed.

STEP 3: WRITING A TITLE THAT GETS FOUND

This is where many people get tripped up—but you don't have to.

Your product title should sound like something someone would actually search for. Think: what would your ideal buyer type into Etsy's search bar if they were looking for your item?

For example:

Good:

> *DAILY SELF-CARE CHECKLIST | PRINTABLE ROUTINE FOR MOMS*

It's clear, includes keywords, and tells the shopper exactly what they're getting.

Not-so-great:

> *MY PDF #1 FINAL UPLOAD*

That might make sense to you—but to someone scrolling through dozens of listings, it means nothing.

So take a second to be specific. Clarity helps you show up in search and helps buyers feel confident in what they're clicking on.

STEP 4: WRITE THE DESCRIPTION

Your product description is one of the most important parts of your listing—and also one of the most overlooked.

Most people won't read every word. They'll skim. That's why your description needs to be clear, concise, and scannable. If it looks like a wall of text, there's a good chance they'll bounce without ever learning what makes your product great.

Use short paragraphs, simple sentences, and highlight important details with bold text (especially for digital items: file type, size, usage, etc.). Think of it like a conversation—friendly, helpful, and easy to follow.

Here's a structure that works:

1. **Intro** – What is this and who is it for?

2. **What's included** – How many pages, formats, sizes, etc.

3. **How to use it** – Print at home? Use digitally?

4. **Why it's useful** – Talk benefits, not just features

5. **Any extras** – Bonus page? Editable fields?

6. **Friendly reminder** – "This is a digital file. No physical item will be shipped".

Also, let's touch on **SEO (Search Engine Optimization)**—because your description helps with that too.

WHAT IS SEO?

SEO is about making your product easier to find when people search for it. The words you use in your description help platforms like Etsy or Gumroad decide whether to show your product in results.

How to use SEO in your description:

• Use your main keywords—more on what those are in the next section—naturally in the first few lines.

- Repeat them 1–2 more times if it makes sense (but don't force it).

- Think about how your customer would search—and write with that in mind.

You're not trying to trick the system. You're just helping the right people find the right thing faster.

A well-written description does two things: it makes the buyer feel confident in what they're getting, and it helps your listing get discovered. Keep it human, helpful, and easy to skim.

Example:

This printable daily self-care checklist is designed for busy moms who want to make space for themselves—even on the craziest days. You'll get a clean, minimalist PDF (8.5 x 11) with easy-to-follow prompts to build your daily routine.

Print it once and reuse it as often as you like—or upload it into a digital planner. Perfect for building consistency without stress.

Bonus: Includes a kid-friendly checklist to do together!

Please note: This is a digital download. No physical product will be shipped.

STEP 5: ADD IMAGES OR MOCKUPS

If you're listing the product you worked on during the first week of this guide, good news—you already created your mockups. Use what you made! Just upload the mockup images you've designed unless you want to improve or update them.

If you're working on a brand-new product, no worries. Go back and review the mockup creation process we walked through earlier (Day 4). Use Canva to build a few clean, scroll-stopping visuals:

- A styled image of the product in context (like on a desk or being used)
- A close-up of one or two sample pages so customers know what they're getting
- Optional: A branded slide with your logo or your product's "look and feel"

Keep it simple, clutter-free, and easy to understand. The goal isn't to show off design tricks—it's to help the buyer see themselves using it.

STEP 6: UPLOAD IT ALL

Follow your platform's prompts:

- Upload your file(s)
- Add product images
- Choose a category
- Add your price and description

If you're using Printify + Etsy:

You'll actually create the listing inside Printify. Once your product is ready:

- **Click "Publish to Etsy"** inside Printify
- The listing will appear in your Etsy shop's drafts
- Then **go to Etsy** to finalize the title, description, tags, pricing, and other listing details
- **Printify automatically syncs** the files and mockups to Etsy—but double-check everything looks right
- **Set your prices** carefully to account for Printify's base cost, Etsy's fees, and your desired profit margin

Give it a quick test run:

After you've hit publish, open up your Etsy listing and take a moment to preview it like a customer would. There's a handy "Preview as customer" button—use it. It's an easy way to spot things like weird formatting, a photo that didn't load, or a small typo that slipped through.

Pro tip: Take a look through Printify's product catalog from time to time. Some items ship faster or offer better profit margins than others. You can also choose from different Print Providers for each product, which gives you a bit more control over cost and quality.

Okay, now let's shift gears and talk about something that can really affect how many people actually find your listing: keywords and tags.

WHAT ARE KEYWORDS?

Keywords are the words and phrases people type into the search bar when they're looking for something. If your product listing includes the right ones, your product has a better chance of showing up in search results.

Why they matter

No matter how beautiful your product is, it won't get found unless you're using words your customers are already searching for. Good keywords help your listing appear in front of the right eyes.

How to find them

- Look at 5–10 similar products on Etsy or Gumroad. What words are showing up again and again in titles and tags?
- Start typing your product type into the Etsy search bar and watch what it auto-suggests—that's what people are actively looking for.
- Use free tools like eRank or Keyword Tool Dominator (for Etsy) to research popular search terms. (both have limited free tiers and budget-friendly paid plans)

How to use them

- Include the strongest keywords in your title and your first sentence of the description.
- Use all available tag slots (Etsy gives you 13) with a mix of broad and specific terms.

- Think like a shopper: What would you type if you were looking for your own product?

Example keywords:

- "daily planner printable"
- "self care checklist"
- "mom life routine template"
- "editable PDF planner"

Use natural language—don't just stack keywords. The listing should still read smoothly.

Once your tags are added and everything looks good: Hit publish.

That's it. Your first listing is live.

Tomorrow we'll talk about getting your first views and clicks. But today—this is a big one. You just moved from "thinking about selling" to actually doing it. That's huge.

More products will come. But for now? One great listing is enough.

- How to choose which product to list first
- How to set a fair starting price
- How to write strong, searchable titles and descriptions
- How to apply SEO and keywords effectively
- How to upload files, images, and details for your listing
- How Printify and Etsy work together (and how to publish properly)

This is your first real listing—congrats! Tomorrow we'll work on how to get that first wave of traffic to your store.

DAY 9: UPLOAD AND FINALIZE LISTING CHECKLIST

- ☐ Choose the product you want to list first
- ☐ Save it in the right format with a clean file name
- ☐ Set your price based on product type and platform fees
- ☐ Write a clear, searchable title
- ☐ Write a strong product description
- ☐ Include SEO keywords naturally in your title and description
- ☐ Upload 2–3 mockup images
- ☐ Publish your file and listing on Etsy or Gumroad
- ☐ If using Printify, create the listing in Printify and click "Publish to Etsy"
- ☐ Finalize the listing details in Etsy (title, tags, description, price)
- ☐ Preview the listing using Etsy's customer view
- ☐ Save your listing link and track it in your product doc

DAY 10: GET YOUR FIRST VIEWS AND CLICKS

You've done it—your first product is live! That's a huge milestone. But now comes the next challenge: getting actual people to see it.

Today is all about visibility. We're not talking about paid ads or complicated launch plans (yet). We're going to focus on a few simple, free, low-pressure ways to start getting attention and traffic to your listing.

STEP 1: SHARE WHERE IT MAKES SENSE

Let's be honest: nobody wants to be the person spamming every group chat with a sales link. The goal here is to **share with intention**, not desperation.

Here are some good starting points:

- Post it on your personal or brand Instagram story (add a little context like "Just launched my first printable!" or "Made this to help fellow busy moms stay organized")
- Share in a relevant Facebook group—if allowed—and be genuine (offer it as a helpful resource)
- Drop the link in your email signature or a group you're active in
- If you've already started a niche-focused Instagram or TikTok account, post it there with a short video or carousel

Pro tip: Add a story highlight or pinned post so your product is always easy to find.

STEP 2: USE PINTEREST TO YOUR ADVANTAGE

Pinterest is basically a visual search engine—and it's free traffic gold if you use it right.

Here's how to get started:

1. Create a free business account on Pinterest (if you haven't yet)

2. Design 1–3 pins in Canva featuring your product (use mockups and keyword-based titles)

3. Add the product link and a short, benefit-driven description

Pins can keep bringing traffic for weeks or even months. Don't skip this one.

STEP 3: BUILD A TINY LAUNCH PLAN

You don't need a giant audience. Just a few people who care. A mini launch plan could look like this:

- **Day 1:** Share your listing on your socials with a personal note (why you made it)
- **Day 2:** Post a behind-the-scenes photo or video

- **Day 3:** Share a user tip or a bonus (like a matching checklist, a companion worksheet, or a quick tip on how to use your product)

- **Day 4:** Ask a question or poll your audience ("What type of planner do you actually use?")

It doesn't have to be perfect—it just has to keep the momentum going.

STEP 4: DON'T JUST POST—ENGAGE

When someone likes, comments, or shares your content—reply. Say thank you. Start a conversation. It builds trust and reminds people there's a real human behind the product.

Even better? Go comment on 3–5 related accounts or posts every day. No selling, just engaging.

This isn't about going viral—it's about being visible.

A QUICK REALITY CHECK BEFORE WE WRAP

Let's be honest: this isn't a "get rich quick" plan. Those don't exist—at least not without risk, luck, or a bank account already stacked with cash. What you're doing is real. It's honest. And it may take time.

Getting that first sale might not happen on Day 1. But the more you invest, the sooner it comes—and by "invest", I mean both time and money. You get to decide how you want to build:

- **Time-rich, budget-tight?** Put in extra effort creating, promoting, and learning. It's slower, but every bit of growth is yours.
- **Cash-ready, short on time?** Invest in ads, freelancers, or pro templates to move quicker—but with financial risk.

Both paths are valid. This guide leans toward the "minimal investment" route so that you can grow steadily without pressure. Later, once you've built your brand and audience, scaling up—or outsourcing—will feel much easier and more natural.

WHAT YOU'VE LEARNED TODAY

- Learned free, beginner-friendly ways to start driving traffic
- Created your first mini visibility plan
- Took the first real steps toward getting your first buyer

Tomorrow we'll talk about what happens after that first sale—including reviews, files, and the customer experience. But for now, just showing up is more than enough. Keep going—you're doing great.

- Research 3–5 Facebook groups, forums, or social spaces where people in your niche hang out. Observe what types of posts get good engagement.

- Brainstorm 2–3 natural, value-driven ways you could introduce your product to those spaces (without being spammy).

- Ask yourself: If you were your ideal customer, what kind of post would catch your attention and make you click?

- Optional: Create one Pinterest pin or IG story to start getting visibility right away.

☐ **Pinterest & Searchable Platforms**

  ☐ Identify 2–3 relevant communities or hashtags

  ☐ Create a Pinterest Business account (if you haven't already)

  ☐ Design 1–3 promotional pins in Canva using mockups and keyword-rich titles

  ☐ Write a short description that explains the benefit or use of your product

  ☐ Link each pin directly to your product listing

  ☐ Post the pins and save them to relevant boards

☐ **Social Media Mini Launch Plan**

  ☐ Share your product on social media with a personal backstory or message

  ☐ Post a behind-the-scenes look (design process, mockup, or concept sketch)

  ☐ Share a bonus tip, alternate use, or companion product suggestion

  ☐ Ask your audience a simple question or create a poll (e.g. "Which design do you like better?")

☐ **Community Outreach & Engagement**

  ☐ Identify 2–3 hashtags or online communities where your audience is active

  ☐ Join and participate in at least one relevant Facebook group, Reddit thread, or niche forum

  ☐ Share a helpful comment or product teaser (following group rules)

  ☐ If allowed, share your video, product story, or mockup in a natural, non-spammy way

☐ Content Sharing & Interaction Boost

- ☐ Reuse your product video or Canva graphic in Stories, Reels, or TikTok
- ☐ Add a call-to-action or question in your caption to encourage responses
- ☐ Respond to any comments or DMs within 24 hours to keep the momentum going
- ☐ Track what kind of content gets the most reactions, saves, or clicks

DAY 11: WHAT HAPPENS AFTER THE FIRST SALE?

That first sale notification will feel like magic—but once it hits, you need to be ready to deliver a great experience. Even if your product is digital and doesn't require shipping, there's still plenty you can do to make a strong first impression and lay the groundwork for a long-term brand.

Today is about understanding what happens behind the scenes, how to handle customer questions, and what to do to turn a buyer into a repeat customer.

STEP 1: MAKE SURE THE FILES ARE ACCESSIBLE

Before you pop the confetti, take a minute to make sure everything went through smoothly on the buyer's end. A great customer experience starts with the download process.

On Etsy—head into your listing manager and confirm that the files are uploaded correctly. Double-check that each one is clearly labeled and easy to find.

Using Gumroad? Test the link yourself—log out or use a different browser to make sure the download process works like it should.

Keep your filenames clean and clear. Avoid things like finaldraft_5_UPDATED_actualFINAL.pdf. Instead, go for something like Daily_Gratitude_Journal_Printable.pdf.

If you're selling a ZIP file, it's a nice touch to include a quick README inside. A short message with usage instructions or a thank-you note can go a long way toward making your product feel polished and personal.

Selling physical products through Printify? There's an option during setup to include a custom thank-you message (card) with the order. It's a small added cost, but it can go a long way in making your package feel special—and memorable.

Bonus tip: If you're on Instagram (or any other platform), include your handle or a QR code inside the file or card. That way, happy buyers can follow you, tag your product in posts, or reach out with feedback.

STEP 2: THINK LIKE A CUSTOMER

Put yourself in their shoes: they clicked, paid, and now they're excited to use your product. Make sure they're not left guessing.

- Was the file what you promised in the listing?
- Were the visuals and layout easy to understand?
- Did it feel smooth, or clunky?

You don't need a fancy system—just a genuine focus on the buyer experience. Even a quick check-in message after purchase (if the platform allows) can make a big difference.

STEP 3: ENCOURAGE A REVIEW (THE RIGHT WAY)

Let's face it—reviews matter. Good reviews matter even more—they build trust and help your product get discovered by more people. But asking for one may feel a little uncomfortable.

The key is to keep it light and genuine. You're not begging—you are just opening the door. Something simple like this can work:

"Hope you're enjoying the download! If it's been helpful, I'd really appreciate a quick review—it makes a big difference for small creators like me."

You can drop this line into the post-purchase message, or even include it at the bottom of your file (or inside your thank-you note if you're selling physical items).

No pressure, no guilt trips—and definitely no bribes (some platforms like Etsy don't allow review incentives). The goal is to remind your buyer that their voice matters, and that behind the product is a real person who appreciates the support.

At the end of the day, great reviews usually come from great experiences. If you've made things smooth, helpful, and a little personal, you've already done most of the work.

STEP 4: WATCH FOR QUESTIONS OR ISSUES

Sometimes customers don't reach out—they just get confused and leave a bad review. To avoid that:

- Make your listing description super clear (we covered this in Day 9)

- Offer easy ways to get in touch

- Monitor your inbox/messages during the first few days after launch

You don't need to babysit every file forever—but checking in during the early stages builds confidence and saves headaches.

WHAT YOU'VE LEARNED TODAY

- How to prep your product so it delivers a great customer experience

- How to follow up professionally

- How to plant the seeds for good reviews

Tomorrow, we'll cover small ways to improve your product and listings after launch—without starting over. You're building something real, and it's already working. Let's keep that momentum going.

☐ **Review your full buyer journey**

Walk through your product's path from purchase to delivery.
Check download links, file names, formatting, and any platform
notifications that go out to buyers.

☐ **Test all digital files**

Open and double-check every PDF, ZIP file, or image
included. Make sure everything opens correctly and looks
polished. Add a README or simple instruction page if needed.

☐ **Include a thoughtful thank-you**

Write a short message of appreciation—either inside the product
file or using your platform's message feature. Optional: Add a
personalized thank-you note in Printify if selling physical goods.

☐ **Add your social handles (or QR code)**

Make it easy for happy customers to follow you or share their
experience by including your Instagram or TikTok handle, or even
a scannable QR code.

☐ **Write or update your FAQ section**

Anticipate common buyer questions and include answers in your
listing or shop FAQ. This could cover file access, printing tips, or
how to use the product.

☐ **Draft a friendly review request**

Come up with one or two short, natural-sounding review
messages that you can reuse across listings or messages. Keep it
casual and appreciative.

☐ Brainstorm ways to encourage reviews

☐ **Place the review message inside your product file (or in a
thank-you card)**

A simple line at the bottom of your PDF or on a thank-you insert like:

"If this brought a little joy or helped you in any way, I'd love it if you left a quick review. It helps more than you know."

☐ Check platform guidelines

Make sure your review messaging follows your platform's rules (e.g., Etsy does not allow incentivized reviews).

DAY 12: IMPROVE WITHOUT STARTING OVER

Your product is live. You've made your first sale (or you're getting close). Now it's time to do what most creators skip: **improve**.

Today we're going to talk about refining your listing based on real-world feedback, even if no one's bought it yet. Small tweaks can make a big difference.

STEP 1: LOOK AT YOUR LISTING LIKE A BUYER WOULD

Today's goal is to give your listing a fresh pair of eyes. Even if it hasn't made a sale yet, a few small adjustments can sometimes be all it takes to boost clicks or spark interest.

Step Into Your Customer's Shoes. Pull up your listing—either on your phone or in a private browser window—and pretend it's the first time you're seeing it.

Ask yourself:

- Does the title instantly tell you what it is?
- Do the images stop the scroll?
- Is it clear what someone's getting without reading too much?
- Are the benefits obvious—or does it sound a little generic?

Now picture this: you're half-watching Netflix, holding a toddler, and scrolling with your thumb. Would this listing still catch your eye? Would you trust it enough to click?

This exercise is about spotting the little things—because sometimes that's where the magic (and missed opportunity) is.

STEP 2: TWEAK YOUR KEYWORDS AND TAGS

Even if your listing is beautiful, the right people won't see it if your tags are off.

• Go to Etsy or Gumroad and search for similar products—what exact words show up?

• Try typing into the search bar and noting what it suggests

• Adjust your tags and even your title to reflect more popular or relevant phrases

You can also test tools like **eRank**, **Marmalead** (for Etsy), or **Keyword Tool Dominator** to help with this.

STEP 3: IMPROVE THE FIRST IMAGE

Your first image is the one that stops the scroll. If it's cluttered, unclear, or low contrast, you're losing potential clicks.

Try one of these upgrades:

• Add a bold title directly onto the image (keep it short)

• Use a clean, mockup background with less clutter

• Zoom in on the most useful part of the product

If you're not sure, make two and ask a friend or post a poll in a niche group.

STEP 4: ADD A LITTLE SOMETHING EXTRA

You don't need a bad review to justify making your product better. Sometimes, adding a small touch—just because—can really make someone's day.

Think about slipping in a bonus page: maybe a quick-start guide, an extra variation of your design, or a simple checklist to help them get the most out of what they've downloaded.

Or maybe the layout could be cleaned up a bit. If something felt "good enough" the first time around, now's your chance to polish it.

And if you haven't already, why not include a short thank-you note inside the file? It could be as easy as a kind message with your Instagram handle or a little coupon code for their next visit.

On Etsy or Gumroad, you can just upload the new version to your original listing. No need to start from scratch—it's a quiet upgrade that adds value without a whole lot of effort.

Made a few upgrades? Don't keep it to yourself.

- Post a quick "before and after" image of the update
- Mention the bonus in a short caption or story ("Hey, I just added a printable tracker to this bundle!")
- Share your link again, but this time focus on what's new or improved

You're not spamming—this is about showing progress. People love seeing creators tweak and grow. It helps them trust that your products will keep getting better over time.

WHAT YOU'VE LEARNED TODAY

Before we wrap up—one quick reminder.

Don't let slow sales or quiet social posts discourage you. Most of us don't start with 10K followers or viral content—and that's okay. Building something real takes time. Keep showing up, share your journey and focus on offering a great experience for your customers.

Someone out there is looking for exactly what you've made—they just haven't found you yet. Be patient, be helpful, and keep learning. The rest will follow.

Now, here's what we covered today:

- How to strengthen your visuals, description, and keywords
- How to improve and relaunch without starting from scratch

Tomorrow, we'll take a step back and look at a few other ways you can earn using AI. After all, we've signed up for quite a few tools—and only tapped into a handful. If you're feeling curious (or if product listings aren't your favorite), there are other creative and meaningful ways to use what you've learned so far to build income online. For today, a little polish goes a long way.

DAY 12: MOTIVATION & MINDSET CHECKLIST

☐ **Take 10 minutes to journal**

Write about how far you've come. What felt easy? What surprised you? What's still a little scary or uncertain?

☐ **Identify 1–2 mindset blocks**

It could be fear of judgment, perfectionism, imposter syndrome, or even procrastination. Call it out—then challenge it.
Reframe it like this:

"I don't know enough" → "I'm learning by doing, and that's how real progress happens."

"What if no one buys it?" → "What if someone does?"

☐ **Write one positive affirmation that feels real**

Not cheesy—something you actually believe (or want to believe). Examples:

"Progress beats perfection."

"I'm building something that matters to me."

"I don't have to be an expert to get started."

☐ **Share a small behind-the-scenes moment**

Post a photo of your messy desk, a screenshot of your Canva draft, or a funny thought from your process. Let your audience see that there's a real person behind the product.

☐ **Celebrate one small win**

It could be finishing your first listing, getting feedback, learning a new tool, or simply showing up every day. Give it the credit it deserves.

☐ **Check in with your 'why'**

Why did you start this? Who are you doing it for? Reconnect with the purpose—it's easy to forget in the middle of the to-do list.

☐ **Give yourself permission to take a break (if needed)**

Sometimes momentum comes from rest, not hustle. If you're burning out, today might be a great day to pause and recharge for the next phase.

DAY 13: USE AI TO START A BLOG THAT BRINGS IN INCOME

You've launched your first product, your shop is up and running—and maybe now you're wondering what else you can do with the tools you've already got installed. One really solid option? Start a blog.

This doesn't mean you need to become a full-time blogger or post every day. Far from it. This is about building a simple, useful blog that either supports your shop—or gives you a totally different way to earn online. It's flexible. You can make it your main focus or treat it like a side channel for traffic.

If you've got a message to share or tips to offer, and you want a space that keeps working for you long after it's posted, blogging might just be your next smart move. And with tools like ChatGPT, Grammarly, and Canva—you're more ready for it than you think.

STEP 1: CHOOSE A BLOG TOPIC YOU CAN BUILD AROUND

Your blog should ideally be connected to your product or audience. Ask yourself:

- What do I know a little more about than the average person?
- What kind of problems do my potential customers have?
- What can I talk about for 10–15 blog posts without getting bored?

If you're selling planners for moms, your blog might be about routines, time-saving tips, or printable hacks. If you're into digital art, your blog could cover AI tools, mockup design tips, or creative process walkthroughs.

STEP 2: USE AI TO OUTLINE AND DRAFT POSTS

Let's say you want to create a blog post but don't know where to start. Try this: open ChatGPT (or Gemini, or Claude—whichever you prefer) and ask for help shaping the basics of your idea. For example:

> *I WANT TO WRITE A BLOG POST CALLED '5 SIMPLE MORNING ROUTINES FOR BUSY MOMS.' CAN YOU HELP ME OUTLINE SECTION TITLES AND 2–3 MAIN POINTS UNDER EACH?*

You'll get a nice basic framework—something you can build on. After that, follow up with:

> *GREAT, NOW HELP ME DRAFT THIS IN A RELAXED, CONVERSATIONAL TONE.*

Here's the part I keep repeating over and over again: Do not copy and paste directly from ChatGPT. People can tell. That generic tone and overly neat phrasing is a huge red flag and the fastest way to lose trust.

The real skill isn't copying text—it's using AI to generate ideas and structure, then putting your voice on top of it. AI is your assistant, not your replacement.

Once you've shaped your draft:

Use free Grammarly browser extension to catch typos, tone mismatches, or awkward phrasing. If you installed it earlier, it should automatically check as you type in Google Docs, Notion, or WordPress.

Don't have it? Try the free version at grammarly.com, or explore alternatives like Hemingway Editor (free in-browser) or Slick Write.

These tools won't write for you, but they'll help you tighten things up and make sure your writing flows naturally.

STEP 3: HELP PEOPLE FIND IT—WITHOUT OVERTHINKING SEO

Let's be honest—SEO can feel a bit overwhelming. But you don't need to be a search engine wizard to make your post discoverable. Just write like a human who's trying to help another human find something useful.

Here's what that looks like:

- Use natural language in your title—something a friend might search, like "quick morning routine for moms"
- Mention the topic early on, especially in the intro

- Write a short summary (under 160 characters) that tells people what the post is about. It shows up under your blog link in search results
- Drop in an image or two. Canva is great for this, or you can grab something from a free site like Pexels

If you're stuck on the summary, ChatGPT can give you a draft. Just don't copy it word-for-word. Take the idea and put your own spin on it—like how you'd explain it to a friend.

STEP 4: GENTLY NUDGE TOWARD A PURCHASE

Once people are reading your post, you've got a chance to turn that attention into action. And no, you don't need to be pushy.

Here are some ways to earn a little from your blog:

- Mention one of your products in a helpful way. For example, "This checklist helped me stick to my morning routine— here's the one I made."
- Add links to tools you actually like and use. If they offer affiliate programs (like Canva or Amazon), sign up and earn a small commission if someone clicks through.
- Offer a little freebie in exchange for an email address—like a mini version of your product. Then you've got a way to stay in touch later.

Blogging doesn't have to be daily. One good post can bring steady traffic for months if it's useful and easy to find. Just keep showing up, one piece at a time.

PRACTICE: YOUR TURN

- Choose one blog topic that fits your product or niche
- Use ChatGPT (or Gemini / Claude) to create an outline and draft
- Clean it up in your own voice
- Add 1–2 product or affiliate links
- If you don't have a blog platform yet, create a free one on Medium, Substack, or your own site via WordPress or Wix

WHAT YOU'VE LEARNED TODAY

- Blogging is still a powerful, passive traffic tool—and AI makes it easier than ever to get started
- You don't need to be a professional writer to create valuable, helpful content
- A simple, well-written blog post can do more than just share ideas—it can quietly promote your store every day

Tomorrow we'll explore affiliate marketing and how to use AI to support that model too. One small step at a time—you're building a digital foundation that can grow with you.

☐ **Pick your platform**

Choose where you'll publish your blog (e.g. Substack, Medium, WordPress, Ghost). Don't overthink—just pick the one that feels easiest for you to start.

☐ **Claim your blog name or title**

Set a clear blog name, headline, or page title that aligns with your brand or niche (you can change this later if needed).

☐ **Write your first post**

Use an AI tool (like ChatGPT) to outline and brainstorm your topic, then write your draft in your own voice.

☐ **Add helpful formatting**

Break up your post with headers, bullet points, bold text, and images so it's easy to skim.

☐ **Include at least one internal link**

Link to your Etsy, Gumroad, or product page in a natural way within the post.

☐ **Add at least one external resource**

Link to a helpful free tool, stat, or article to build credibility and value.

☐ **Include a call-to-action (CTA)**

At the end of your post, invite readers to check out your product, download your freebie, or leave a comment.

☐ **Optimize for search**

Add a short, clear meta description (under 160 characters) and make sure your post includes a few natural keywords.

☐ **Proofread and edit**

Use a tool like Grammarly or Hemingway Editor to clean up typos and improve flow.

☐ **Hit publish!**

Don't wait for it to be perfect—get your first post live and learn as you go.

☐ **Share it on social media**

Post the link on Instagram, Pinterest, Threads, or wherever your audience hangs out. Add a personal note about why you wrote it.

☐ **Track your performance**

Monitor traffic, likes, comments, or clicks over the next few days. Use it as feedback—not judgment.

DAY 14: START EARNING WITH AFFILIATE MARKETING (AND AI HELP)

Maybe you're not quite ready to create another product, or maybe you're just looking for a way to earn while your shop or blog is still picking up steam (or, maybe you are just testing the water to see what goods are the most popular with the customers). That's where affiliate marketing comes in—it's one of the most approachable ways to start earning online.

In simple terms, affiliate marketing is recommending something you've tried or liked. If someone clicks your unique link and buys it, you get a small commission. You don't need to create the product, manage orders, or do any customer service. It's all about sharing what you already use or believe in.

Let's use Amazon as a quick example. If you sign up for their affiliate program (Amazon Associates), you can share links to products—books, tools, tech, whatever fits your audience. Let's say you're reading this book. If you enjoy it and want to tell others about it, you could record a short TikTok, post a photo with a caption, or write a blog review. Include your affiliate link, and if someone buys the book—or anything else in that shopping session—you'll get a percentage of that sale.

And just to be clear, this isn't me hinting you should promote this book (although hey, if you want to, I won't stop you). This is just a simple, real-life example you can wrap your head around.

Amazon typically pays up to 10%, depending on the category. So if someone clicks your link and buys $100 worth of items, you might earn up to $10, no extra effort required.

Of course, Amazon isn't the only option. Here are a few other platforms that offer solid affiliate programs:

- o **ShareASale** – access to affiliate programs from hundreds of merchants. Commission rates vary by partner, but generally range from 5% to 20%.
- o **Impact** – used by major brands like Canva, Skillshare, and more. Rates vary by brand, but many offer between 10% to 30% commissions.
- o **CJ Affiliate** (formerly Commission Junction) – a long-established platform with high-quality partners and custom rates, often 5%–15% depending on the merchant and product type

Now let's walk through how to get started.

STEP 1: PICK A NICHE YOU'RE NATURALLY DRAWN TO

If you're going to recommend something, it should be something you'd talk about even if no one paid you. That's your best bet for earning trust—and commissions. Think about where your own interests already live:

- Are you the person always showing others how to organize their digital files or planners?

- Do friends come to you for gift ideas, productivity hacks, or creative tools?

- Is there a product you've already used, loved, and told five people about?

The goal isn't to pick the "most profitable" topic—it's to choose one you'll still enjoy a month from now. Your enthusiasm will come through and that's what gets clicks.

STEP 2: SIGN UP FOR AFFILIATE PROGRAMS THAT FIT

Once you know what you'd actually feel good recommending, it's time to sign up for a few programs that match your niche. Here are some beginner-friendly ones that work especially well for creatives and digital shop owners:

- **Creative Fabrica**
  Great for printables, font bundles, and design elements. If you use their stuff already, this one's a no-brainer.
- **Gumroad**
  They let you earn a cut by promoting other people's digital products—super useful if you're not ready to make your own yet.
- **Amazon Associates**
  Yes, commissions are small, but if you're linking to books, planners, or tools your audience already uses, it adds up.
- **Design Bundles / Font Bundles**
  Perfect if your people love templates, SVGs, or graphics. You'll probably find something you'd buy yourself.

- ○ **ShareASale or ClickBank**
  These are affiliate networks where you can browse loads of products and brands. A bit more setup, but they give you options.

Pro tip: You don't need to join ten programs. Start with one or two that make sense for your content, and go from there.

STEP 3: USE AI TO GET UNSTUCK

If you ever find yourself staring at a blank screen, AI tools like ChatGPT can seriously help. Ask for a list of points to include in a tool comparison or get a basic structure for a blog post—just to kick things off. For example:

> *HEY, I'M COMPARING ADOBE EXPRESS VS CANVA PRO FOR DIGITAL PLANNER DESIGN—WHAT SHOULD I TALK ABOUT?*

You'll probably get something useful—but don't stop there. That's your starting line. Go back through and add your personal take: what you liked, what annoyed you, what actually worked in real life. Sincere feedback always wins.

STEP 4: JUST BE UPFRONT ABOUT AFFILIATE LINKS

If you're sharing a link that might earn you a small commission - mention it. Keep it simple and honest. Something like:

> *HEADS UP—SOME OF THESE LINKS ARE AFFILIATE LINKS. THAT MEANS IF YOU CLICK AND BUY, I MIGHT GET A SMALL THANK-YOU FROM THE COMPANY. IT DOESN'T COST YOU ANYTHING EXTRA*

That's really all it takes. No need to sound overly formal or apologetic—people are cool with it as long as you're clear. And honestly, folks are way more likely to trust you if it feels like a real recommendation, not a sneaky sales pitch. Just share what you genuinely like and why.

PRACTICE: YOUR TURN

- Think about a product, app, or tool you actually enjoy using—maybe something you've mentioned to friends or use regularly in your creative work.
- Look up their affiliate program and sign up (it usually only takes a few minutes).
- Write a short caption or blog post recommending it— something casual and helpful, not salesy.
- Add your referral link, and keep an eye on your stats (most programs give you a dashboard to track clicks and commissions).

WHAT YOU'VE LEARNED TODAY

- You learned that affiliate marketing can be a chill, low-effort way to earn—without having to create something new from scratch.

- You saw how AI tools can help you organize your thoughts and speed up the writing process.

- Most importantly, you were reminded that trust matters. People appreciate real opinions more than polished pitches.

Up next: We'll look at how to offer simple services powered by AI—plus where to list them so people can start hiring you.

DAY 14: AFFILIATE MARKETING CHECKLIST

☐ Pick your focus:
  ☐ Decide what niche or type of product you want to promote (e.g. tools for printable design, AI apps, wellness printables, etc.)
  ☐ Choose a platform you'll use to share (Instagram, blog, YouTube, Pinterest, etc.)
☐ Research affiliate programs:
  ☐ Sign up for one or more programs that match your niche (e.g. Amazon Associates, ShareASale, Creative Fabrica, Adobe, Rakuten, Impact, etc.)
  ☐ Read their terms—check rules about disclosure, payouts, and where you can post links
☐ Choose a product you've used or genuinely like:
  ☐ Pick 1–2 items you already use or would confidently recommend
  ☐ Grab your unique affiliate links from the program dashboard
☐ Create helpful, non-pushy content:
  ☐ Write a mini review, tutorial, or comparison post
  ☐ Share a tip or story that includes the product naturally
  ☐ Post it to your chosen platform (social media, blog, email, etc.)
☐ Add visuals if possible
☐ Add a clear disclosure

Example: "This post contains affiliate links, which means I may earn a commission if you purchase—at no extra cost to you."

- ☐ Track performance:
    - ☐ Log into your affiliate dashboard and review click or commission stats
    - ☐ Note which posts or platforms are bringing the most traffic
- ☐ Optional: Build on it
    - ☐ Create a "tools I love" page on your blog
    - ☐ Turn the content into a carousel or Reel for more reach
    - ☐ Experiment with link-in-bio tools like Later, Beacons, or Linktree to organize multiple affiliate links

WEEK 2 RECAP: YOU LAUNCHED YOUR FIRST PRODUCT

Week 2 was where things got real. You stopped planning and started publishing—putting your work out there in a way that takes guts and follow-through. That kind of leap deserves some credit.

Let's pause and look back at everything you managed to push through:

You launched your first real product – You went from an idea in your head to a live listing—images, description, pricing, the whole deal. It's no longer just a plan—it's real and out there. And now it's out in the world.

You wrote for real people—not algorithms – Whether it was your product description or a caption for your social post, you focused on being helpful, clear, and human.

You took your first shot at marketing – You shared. You posted. Maybe you made a pin or tested a reel. And if you didn't yet, you at least thought through where and how you'll show up.

You paid attention to the customer experience – From download to follow-up, you started thinking like someone running a business—not just someone listing a file.

You learned to adjust without tossing it all – You reviewed your listing, made small tweaks, and saw that "good enough to start" doesn't mean "done forever".

You explored new income paths – Blogging and affiliate marketing are no longer mysterious. You now know how they fit into your bigger picture, whether you use them now or later.

If Week 1 was your setup phase, Week 2 was the moment you showed up. You didn't just think like a creator—you acted like one.

Now we're going to take all that energy and start building something that lasts. Week 3 is where it starts to feel like a real business.

WEEK 3:

SCALING & AUTOMATING

DAY 15: USE AI TO OFFER SERVICES ONLINE (EVEN AS A BEGINNER)

Not in the mood to build a blog or wait for affiliate sales? Want faster feedback, quicker payments, and something you can offer right now? Freelance services might be the path for you.

With everything you've already learned (and all the tools you've signed up for), you can start offering simple, valuable services—even if you're new. Today we'll explore how to use AI to boost your skills, speed up delivery, and confidently post your first gig.

STEP 1: WHAT CAN YOU OFFER?

Here are some beginner-friendly services that work well with what you've already been doing:

- **Content writing and editing** – Great for people who enjoy putting ideas into words. Use AI to brainstorm or organize your thoughts faster, then shape the final copy yourself.
- **Social media content** – Many small brands would love help writing Instagram captions, prepping Reels scripts, or planning their weekly posts.
- **Canva-based design** – You can create planners, checklists, workbooks, or even branded Pinterest pins for others.
- **Prompt bundles** – Believe it or not, people pay for ready-made prompts for tools like ChatGPT, Midjourney, or Claude—

especially in niche areas like journaling, parenting, or creative writing.

- **Basic SEO help** – If you've started exploring keyword tools like eRank or Ubersuggest, you can help bloggers or shop owners optimize their listings.

Pick something you're familiar with—ideally something you already know how to do or feel confident learning quickly. Clients are hiring you for a professional result, not just for running a tool. That means delivering clean, helpful work—not guessing and hoping it passes.

Start small. Focus on clear outcomes. This doesn't have to be your forever service—it's just a smart way to get paid while building your confidence and portfolio.

STEP 2: USE AI TO SPEED UP YOUR WORKFLOW

Let's be honest—working with clients takes time. Between brainstorming, drafts, edits, and the final polish, it can add up. That's where AI tools come in handy. They don't replace your skills, but they can help you move faster and stay organized.

For example, if you're writing content:

- Use ChatGPT to help you think through headlines or map out a structure.

- Let it draft a rough version, then rewrite it in your own words to sound like you.

- Run the final copy through Grammarly (or even just read it aloud) to catch anything that needs cleaning up.

If you're doing design work:

- Ask ChatGPT to help you come up with a product name or write a quick explainer.
- Use Canva to build your layout—just drag, drop, tweak, and go.
- When a client gives feedback, AI can help you reword things or adjust layout ideas without starting from scratch.

It's not about doing less—it's about doing the creative stuff faster so you can take on more work, or just finish earlier in the day.

STEP 3: WHERE TO OFFER WHAT YOU DO

When you're just starting out, you don't need a fancy website or a polished portfolio to land your first job. Sites like Fiverr are perfect for dipping your toes in—you can post a simple gig, set your own prices, and get your first few clients. Upwork takes a little more setup (you'll need to create a profile and apply to jobs), but it tends to attract clients looking for longer-term help. And if you're curious, platforms like Contra or PeoplePerHour are worth checking out too—less traffic, but also less competition.

As for your listing, keep it simple and real. Something like:

> *I'LL WRITE A 500-WORD BLOG POST, POWERED BY AI TOOLS—BUT 100% REVIEWED AND REFINED BY ME*

Be open, transparent and sincere in your description. You're using tools to help you work faster, but you're the one fine-tuning and shaping the final result. No one's paying for a robot response—they're hiring you for your thinking, editing, and ability to make sure it all makes sense.

If you don't have a portfolio yet, no problem. Create a sample or two and upload those instead. Try offering different price options. For example, a basic gig—one with basic turnaround, and a "premium" one with faster turnaround, extra polish and/or added features. It shows flexibility and gives people choices.

STEP 4: ACT LIKE A PRO (EVEN IF YOU'RE NEW)

You don't need years of experience to leave a good impression. Respond to messages in a timely manner and clearly. Stick to your deadlines. Double-check your work before hitting send. These little things go a long way, especially at the start.

Think of each job as practice. Even the small ones help you get better, build confidence, and earn positive reviews—which matter more than you might think when you're just starting out.

- Pick one service you'd actually feel good doing—maybe something you've helped a friend with before or would enjoy learning more about.

- Write a rough version of your gig title and description. Keep it simple and clear.

- If it makes sense for your service (like design), create a sample or two in Canva just to show what you can do.

- Look at a few real listings on Fiverr or Upwork. What do you like? What would you do differently? Take notes.

WHAT YOU'VE LEARNED TODAY

- Freelancing is a solid way to start making money—especially when you use tools like AI to help move things along faster

- People hire freelancers because they want something done well. You don't need decades of experience, but you do need to know what you're doing.

- If you're still new, that's okay—everyone starts somewhere. You can offer entry-level pricing while you build your portfolio. Be open with your clients about your current skill level if needed and always aim to deliver your best.

- Sites like Fiverr or Upwork can help you get started without needing a huge audience or your own website. It's more about showing up, doing the work and being consistent.

Tomorrow we'll take things further and talk about growing an email list—so you can start connecting with people who want to hear from you directly.

DAY 15: FREELANCE SERVICES CHECKLIST

☐ Brainstorm 2–3 services you could realistically offer using tools you already know (like Canva, Grammarly, ChatGPT, etc.)

☐ Choose one to start with—ideally something that feels comfortable or familiar

☐ Research similar gigs on Fiverr, Upwork, or PeoplePerHour to see what others are offering and how they describe it

☐ Write a clear and honest gig title that explains exactly what you're offering

☐ Draft a compelling description that outlines what the client will get, how you'll deliver it, and any turnaround time

☐ Decide on a starting price that reflects your current skill level (entry-level is totally fine as long as the quality is solid)

☐ Create at least one portfolio sample (a writing clip, mockup design, checklist, etc.)—even if it's made just for practice

☐ Add relevant tags and categories so people can find your service

☐ Set clear expectations for delivery time, number of revisions, and communication style

☐ Publish your first gig on Fiverr, Upwork, or another platform

☐ Bonus: Draft a simple outreach message you can use to apply for jobs (especially on platforms like Upwork)

If you've made it this far, you've already done the hard part: building something worth sharing. Now it's time to think about how you stay in touch with people who care—and turn one-time visitors into future customers.

That's where email comes in.

You don't need a massive list to get started. In fact, a small, engaged group of people who've said, "Hey, I'm interested in what you're making", is more powerful than thousands of passive followers.

Today we'll break down how to start an email list, how to get your first signups, and how to use AI to make the process a whole lot easier.

STEP 1: PICK AN EMAIL PLATFORM (FREE IS FINE TO START)

Here are a few solid beginner options:

- o **Mailerlite** – free plan includes up to 1,000 subscribers, drag-and-drop builder
- o **ConvertKit** – great for creators; simple automations, free up to 1,000 subscribers
- o **MailerSend** – newer, but clean design and user-friendly interface
- o **Substack** – more blog-style, but super simple and totally free

Sign up for one and poke around. You don't need to learn every feature—just focus on a few key things:

- **Create a form or landing page.** A landing page is a single-purpose web page (usually provided by your email-list provider) where people sign up to your subscription, newsletter or join your list. Unlike a full website, it doesn't have multiple sections or tabs—it's just a place to explain what someone gets in return for signing up. This is where your audience will land when they click on your signup link from Instagram, Etsy or inside one of your products.
- **Set up a welcome email.** Welcome email is a message someone gets automatically after joining your list. It's your first impression. Use it to say thank you, share the promised freebie or offer and let them know what to expect from you moving forward.
- **View your subscriber list** – This is where you can see everyone who's signed up. Over time, this list becomes a key part of your business. These people chose to stay connected. Unlike social media followers, you actually own this list—it can't be taken away by an algorithm shift or platform change.

That said, **treat this list with care**. Depending on where you live (or where your subscribers are), you'll need to follow certain data protection laws—like **GDPR** in the EU or **CAN-SPAM** in the US. Never sell or share your list with third parties, and don't spam people with pushy sales emails. Always be upfront about what they're signing up for, and make it easy to unsubscribe. These are real people trusting you with their info, and respecting that trust is good for business—and just the right thing to do.

STEP 2: OFFER A REASON TO SUBSCRIBE

People don't just sign up for fun—they want a reason. Give them one.

Here are some low-effort, high-value ideas:

• A free download (like a printable checklist, maze or mini planner)

• A discount code or early access to your next product

• A quick-start guide or how-to PDF

• A short story or behind-the-scenes look at your "production" process

Ask yourself: what would you want from a creator like you?

STEP 3: USE CHATGPT TO WRITE YOUR WELCOME MESSAGE

Don't overthink this. Just make it sound like you. Here's a prompt to start with:

> *WRITE A SHORT, FRIENDLY WELCOME EMAIL FOR PEOPLE WHO SIGNED UP FOR A FREE PRINTABLE PLANNER. KEEP IT CASUAL AND CONVERSATIONAL.*

You'll get a starting draft. Now edit it—trim anything that sounds weird or generic, and make sure it actually sounds like you're writing to a real person.

End with something like:

> *P.S. YOU CAN ALWAYS HIT REPLY AND TELL ME*
> *WHAT KIND OF TOOLS OR CONTENT YOU'RE*
> *LOOKING FOR. I ACTUALLY READ EVERY*
> *RESPONSE.*

That one line makes a big difference.

STEP 4: LINK YOUR FORM WHERE IT MATTERS

You can't just build a signup form and hope people find it. Add it to:

- Your Etsy announcement or shop banner (link it in your bio if possible)
- Your Instagram bio
- Your blog sidebar or post footer
- Inside your product files (e.g., "Want more like this? Grab your free bonus here".)

Just make it easy and natural. If you're offering something helpful, people will say yes.

- Choose one email platform and create a free account
- Draft a simple welcome message using ChatGPT
- Create a signup form and link it somewhere your audience already visits

WHAT YOU'VE LEARNED TODAY

- Email is still one of the most personal, reliable ways to build a long-term audience
- AI can make setup and writing easier—but you still need your voice in it
- You don't need a huge list to start—just one person who wants to hear from you again

Tomorrow, we'll dig into automation—how to save time, stay consistent, and build systems that support your growth (without babysitting them).

DAY 16: BUILD AN EMAIL LIST CHECKLIST

☐ **Choose and sign up for an email marketing platform**
(e.g. MailerLite, ConvertKit, MailerSend, or Substack)

☐ **Create a simple signup form or landing page**
Include a short description of what subscribers will get (freebie, tips, exclusive updates, etc.)

☐ **Set up your subscriber group or list segment**
Keep it organized from the start—name it something like "Freebie Signups" or "Newsletter List"

☐ **Draft a welcome email**
Introduce yourself, thank them for signing up, share your freebie if applicable and let them know what to expect

☐ **Automate your welcome email**
Set it to send immediately after someone joins your list

☐ Link your signup form in key places
- ☐ Instagram bio or Linktree
- ☐ Etsy product file or thank-you page
- ☐ Blog sidebar or footer
- ☐ Pinterest pin or video description

☐ **Test your signup flow**
Use a second email to sign up and check that everything works: the landing page, the confirmation, and the welcome message

☐ **Add a privacy note or disclaimer (optional but recommended)**
Let people know how their data will be used and link to your privacy policy if you have one

☐ **Avoid spam triggers**
Use friendly, clear subject lines and don't overload emails with links or all-caps wording

☐ **Plan your next 2–3 emails**

Think in terms of value: a helpful tip, a product spotlight, or a behind-the-scenes update

DAY 17: AUTOMATE YOUR ADMIN TASKS WITH AI AND SMART TOOLS

Let's be honest—admin work isn't the funnies part of running a business. Scheduling posts, responding to messages, sending the same email ten times... it adds up. But the good news is that you don't have to do it all manually.

Today we'll talk about the tools that will help you create simple automations, that free up your time and keep your business moving, even when you're not actively online.

STEP 1: IDENTIFY WHAT YOU'RE REPEATING

Think about the little tasks that keep popping up:

- Posting content on a schedule
- Sending follow-up emails
- Answering the same questions in DMs or email
- Uploading products or sending files after purchase

If you've done something more than three times this week—it's a great candidate for automation.

One of the best ways to save time? Use tools that already "speak" to each other.

Two popular services can help connect the apps you're using:

o **Zapier** — It links everything from Google Sheets to Instagram to Gmail (and way more). Their free plan gives you a handful of automations, and you can upgrade later if you need more.
zapier.com

o **Make** (formerly Integromat) — Works like Zapier but gives you a more visual, drag-and-drop setup. It's also budget-friendly and   beginner-friendly.
make.com

If you're feeling a little intimidated—don't be. This isn't about creating complicated systems or learning to code. It's just about helping your tools pass info between each other so you're not stuck doing it manually.

Here's how that might look in real life:

• Someone signs up for your freebie → they get tagged in MailerLite → their email is backed up automatically to a Google Sheet

• A buyer fills out your feedback form → they get a thank-you email with a discount code

- You post a new video on YouTube → a quick teaser gets shared to your Instagram story, and the video title gets logged in your Notion board

You're not replacing Etsy or MailerLite's built-in functions—you're just adding a few shortcuts to make your systems run smoother behind the scenes.

Once you set it up and test it, the automation does the work. You can spend more time creating and less time copying and pasting.

STEP 3: SAVE TIME WITH AI-POWERED DRAFTS

AI won't handle customer service for you (unless you run your own website and use an AI-powered chat-bot, but even in this case it's mostly a starting point than a full-fledged customer support), but it can absolutely help you move faster.

Here's how:

- Use ChatGPT (or Gemini / Claude) to write draft replies for messages you get often—like refund requests, order updates, thank-you notes or FAQ responses
- Save them somewhere easy to access: a Google Doc, Notion page or even inside your email platform's "canned responses" or template folder

- When it's time to reply, grab the relevant draft, tweak it to fit the specific situation and hit send—no more typing everything from scratch every time

And if you're regularly writing captions or promo posts:

- Use ChatGPT (or Gemini / Claude) to generate a batch of post ideas and captions
- Store them in a spreadsheet, Notion or your social media scheduler
- Edit lightly before scheduling to make sure they sound like you

This way you're still in control of your voice and tone, but the heavy lifting is already done.

STEP 4: SCHEDULE WHAT YOU CAN

Use tools like:

- **Later**, **Buffer**, or **Metricool** for social media
- **Mailerlite** or **ConvertKit** for email drip campaigns

Scheduling tools help you post consistently—even when life gets busy. You can still show up online without being online.

- Make a list of 3–5 admin tasks you do over and over
- Choose one to automate with Zapier or Make
- Draft 2–3 message or email templates with ChatGPT
- Schedule at least one piece of content for the week ahead

- Automations aren't just for tech people—they're for tired people who need more time
- AI can speed up your writing, responses, and content creation
- You don't have to be online 24/7 to keep your business moving

Tomorrow we'll talk about building your brand and using AI to help you become known for what you do—not just what you sell.

☐ **Identify 3 Repetitive Admin Tasks You Handle Weekly**
Think about anything you do more than once a week—sending thank-you emails, tracking sales, logging customer messages, copying content between platforms, etc.

☐ **Pick One Task to Automate with Zapier or Make**
Choose something simple to start with (e.g., adding new email subscribers to a Google Sheet or sending a confirmation email after a form is submitted).

→ Sign up for Zapier or Make if you haven't already

→ Browse their templates for ideas if you're stuck

☐ **Map Out the Workflow Before You Build It**
Write down the trigger (e.g., "Someone fills out my Typeform") and the action ("Send them a welcome email + save their name to a backup list").

☐ **Test Your Automation to Make Sure It Works**
Use the platform's testing tool to run through the full process before relying on it. Double-check formatting and links.

☐ **Draft 2–3 Message Templates Using ChatGPT**
These can be reused again and again. Try:

    ☐ A thank-you message
    ☐ A follow-up after a purchase
    ☐ A reminder or check-in message for inactive users

☐ **Store Your Templates in One Place**
Keep them in Notion, Google Docs or another easy-access spot so you can copy/paste or automate them later.

☐ Set a Weekly Review Reminder

Automations aren't "set and forget" forever. Create a 10-minute check-in once a week to confirm everything's running smoothly and nothing is broken.

You've got a store. You've launched products. You've even explored other ways to earn. Now let's talk about something that makes it all stick: your brand.

Branding isn't just about picking a nice font or choosing some colors that look good together. It's really about how people remember you. What comes to mind when someone sees your product? What kind of vibe do they get when they scroll past one of your posts?

Start by thinking about what you actually want to be known for. Not just in a business-y way, but in a real human way. What do you care about when you're creating? Who are you making things for? If someone bought one of your products, what would you want them to say about it after using it?

If it's hard to put into words, don't worry—you're not alone. This is where AI can actually help you sound more like... you. Open ChatGPT and try something like:

> *I CREATE COLORFUL PRINTABLE PLANNERS FOR BUSY MOMS. I WANT MY BRAND VOICE TO FEEL FRIENDLY, SMART, AND HONEST. CAN YOU DESCRIBE IT AND HELP ME WRITE A SHORT BIO I CAN USE ON SOCIAL MEDIA?*

You'll get something you can tweak, refine, and make your own. Pull bits of it into your shop description, your About Me section, or even your product listings. Use it anywhere people meet your brand for the first time.

Once you've got a feel for your voice, let's talk visuals. You don't need a fancy brand agency or some complicated style guide. Just pick 2–3 brand colors you love and 1–2 fonts that feel clean and consistent. Tools like Coolors.co can help you find the perfect palette, and Canva is great for testing out font combos. If you want to keep everything in one place, make a simple brand board in Canva—colors, fonts, maybe your logo, and a few notes on the tone or mood you want to stick with.

Here's the part most people miss: consistency beats complexity. You don't have to be on every platform. Just pick one or two where your people are hanging out and show up regularly. Post in your brand voice. Share the behind-the-scenes stuff. Let people in on what you're building, what's working, and even what's not. The more human you are, the more memorable your brand becomes.

If you've been posting without much structure, this is your chance to pause and bring some clarity into it. Try rewriting an Instagram caption or Etsy listing to better match the tone you want. Even small changes can make a big difference in how your work is received.

Branding doesn't mean becoming someone you're not. It means leaning into who you already are—and making sure your audience can recognize it, too.

- Use ChatGPT (or Gemini / Claude) to help put your brand personality into words

- Choose 2–3 brand colors and 1–2 fonts you'll use going forward

- Create a simple brand board in Canva

- Update one social post or product listing to better reflect your voice

WHAT YOU'VE LEARNED TODAY

Your brand is the part people remember. It's not just about looking polished—it's about being consistent, relatable, and real. And when your branding feels like you, people are way more likely to trust you, follow along, and come back.

Tomorrow we'll talk about how to gather and share real feedback, build credibility, and show your audience what makes your work worth paying attention to.

☐ Use ChatGPT (or Gemini / Claude) to Shape Your Brand Voice

☐ **Choose Your Brand Colors (2–3 Core Tones)**

Select colors that reflect your vibe (e.g., muted neutrals for calm, bright tones for energy, pastels for softness)

→ Use a free tool like Coolors.co to generate a palette

→ Tip: Save your hex codes (e.g., #F6C1B5) so you can copy/paste them later into Canva or Etsy

☐ **Pick 1–2 Fonts That Match Your Style**

Choose one for headlines and one for body text. Keep it readable, even on small screens.

→ Try font pairings on Fontpair or test them in Canva

→ Use free Google Fonts or fonts included in Canva's free plan to keep it simple

☐ **Make a Simple Brand Board in Canva**

Create a one-page brand board with:
      ☐ Your logo or shop name
      ☐ Chosen colors
      ☐ Font names and samples
      ☐ A few inspiration images or mockups

→ Save it as a visual reference for your product design and content creation

☐ **Update One Listing or Social Post to Match Your Brand**

Pick a product or Instagram post and:

☐ Adjust the text to match your voice
☐ Update the fonts and colors to your new palette
☐ Swap in branded mockups if you have them
This keeps your customer experience consistent and memorable.

☐ **Optional: Create a Style Guide Document**

Not required, but useful if you want to grow your team or keep things consistent over time.

→ Include tone of voice, visual style, do's and don'ts, and example phrases or posts

DAY 19: BUILD CREDIBILITY AND SHOW YOUR WORK

At this point, you've got products, a store, and a growing sense of your brand. But one of the best ways to gain trust—and stand out—is to show people the process, not just the polish.

You don't need a resume or a huge portfolio. What people really want to see is that you know what you're doing, you care about your work, and you're paying attention to your audience.

So today we're going to talk about how to gather proof, share what you're learning, and build confidence in what you offer—without having to say, "I'm an expert".

Start with something simple: a screenshot of a customer review, a kind message someone sent, or even your own honest reflection on how far you've come since Day 1. Post it with a short caption—something like, "Just got this message from someone who downloaded my planner last week. It made my day".

These tiny moments are what help people feel connected to your work. And if you're just starting and don't have feedback yet? Share your progress. Document the journey. Post a side-by-side of your first design and a recent one. Show a messy sketch that turned into something finished. People love a before-and-after—and they love creators who are real about the work in progress.

You can also use this moment to build in some structure: create a "social proof" folder. Save screenshots of reviews, kind DMs, or helpful feedback in one place so it's easy to reference later. If you're using AI to help create, you can even ask ChatGPT:

> *CAN YOU HELP ME WRITE A SHORT CAPTION TO GO WITH A REVIEW I JUST RECEIVED ON ETSY? IT WAS ABOUT HOW HELPFUL MY PRINTABLE WAS. KEEP IT WARM, FRIENDLY, AND ABOUT 2–3 LINES*

And don't forget case studies. If someone used your product and got a great result—helped their kid stay organized, got their first sale, made their week easier—turn that into a short story. No need to get fancy. A simple paragraph or quote can go a long way. Even better if you include a visual (a screenshot, a testimonial graphic, or a quick Canva-made slide).

The more you share, the easier it becomes for new people to trust you. It's not about proving you're perfect—it's about showing that you care, that you listen, and that your products actually help.

PRACTICE: YOUR TURN

- Save 1–3 examples of feedback, comments, or small wins
- Share one of them in a story, post, or product listing update
- If you don't have customer feedback yet, post a behind-the-scenes or progress snapshot
- Ask ChatGPT to help you write a caption or summary for it

People don't connect with faceless brands. They connect with stories, honesty, and proof that someone out there actually used—and liked—what you made. You don't need to be an expert. You just need to be visible and real.

Tomorrow, we'll look at how to make your work more passive and scalable—so you can keep growing without working 24/7.

☐ **Gather Social Proof**

Go through your messages, DMs, reviews, or emails and:

- ☐ Screenshot or copy 1–3 positive messages, comments, or reactions from real people
- ☐ Save them in a "Testimonials" or "Social Proof" folder for easy access later
- ☐ If you don't have customer feedback yet, use early engagement (poll responses, likes, shares, etc.) or beta tester quotes

☐ Choose One to Share Publicly

- ☐ Turn a kind message or review into **a quote post, Instagram story, or Pinterest pin** (remember, not everyone would want their name to be shared publicly - always anonymize sensitive info or ask permission if sharing names or screenshots)
- ☐ Use Canva to make a clean visual with the quote + your product name or logo

☐ Use AI to Draft a Friendly Caption or Story Blurb

☐ Reflect on What the Feedback Tells You

- ☐ Was the person excited, surprised, grateful?
- ☐ What part of the product stood out most?
- ☐ Could their words inspire a new post, feature, or bonus? Jot down 2–3 thoughts in your content doc or idea tracker

☐ Add a Feedback Section to Your Product Page (Optional)

- ☐ If you're selling through Gumroad or Etsy, consider updating your listing with a great quote or "what customers are saying" section. This builds trust for future buyers and highlights the product's impact

☐ Start a "Happy Folder" for Yourself

    ☐ Keep a personal folder of kind words, wins, and screenshots

    ☐ It's a great morale booster on slow days and a reminder that your work is making a difference

You've spent the past few weeks building, sharing, and showing up. Now it's time to talk about something every creator dreams of—earning while you sleep (or at least while you take a day off). Passive income sounds like magic, but in reality, it just means setting up systems that work without needing you to be online every hour.

The truth? Most passive income still takes upfront work. But once it's running, it frees you up to focus on creating more, experimenting, or taking real breaks.

Let's look at a few simple ways to start building these systems.

1. Schedule and repurpose your best content. You don't have to create something new every day. Look back at what's already worked—an Instagram post, a blog article, an email that got replies—and reuse it.

- Turn a carousel into a reel
- Turn an old email tip into a social caption
- Schedule your content in batches using Later, Buffer, or Metricool

Use AI to help rephrase or adapt it to fit different platforms or formats. You're not cheating—you're being smart with your time.

2. Bundle and repackage your products. If you've created multiple smaller products, see if they can be grouped together into a themed bundle. Maybe:

- 3 printable worksheets become a mini toolkit

- A maze, a coloring sheet, and a planner page become a "Mom & Kid Quiet Time Pack"

Then sell it as a slightly higher-ticket item. This not only increases your product's value but gives customers more reasons to buy from you again.

3. Automate the delivery and follow-up. Tools like Mailerlite, ConvertKit or Gumroad can:

- Deliver your product auto-magically after purchase

- Send a follow-up email with a "thank you" note or bonus

- Ask for a review or invite your customers to join your email list

You can write these once, tweak them with ChatGPT and let them run in the background.

4. Consider a low-lift digital subscription. This isn't for everyone, but if you like creating regularly—printables, templates, guides—you might experiment with:

- A monthly $5 bundle

- A Patreon-style membership with perks

- A Notion template club

Just be honest with yourself: only do this if you know you'll enjoy it. The best subscriptions are the ones that feel fun and light to manage.

PRACTICE: YOUR TURN

- Pick one piece of content to recycle or schedule for next week

- Review your existing products—can you bundle 2–3 into something new?

- If you haven't already, set up an automated thank-you or follow-up email in your platform

- Think about whether a monthly subscription or digital club fits your style

WHAT YOU'VE LEARNED TODAY

Passive income isn't truly "hands off"—but it is freedom-friendly. It's about putting your best stuff to work on repeat, so you're not always chasing the next thing. You've built the pieces. Now it's time to let them work together.

Tomorrow we'll close it all out with a reflection, a celebration, and a plan to grow from here.

☐ Brainstorm a subscription or digital club idea

☐ Repurpose One Piece of Old Content

    ☐ Find a past blog post, social caption, carousel, or video

    ☐ Turn it into a new format (e.g., blog → email series, video → Reels, post → lead magnet)

    ☐ Add a **call to action** linking to your shop, freebie, or product

☐ Bundle Two (or More) Existing Products

    ☐ Look for digital products that naturally fit together (e.g., planner + tracker, quiz + workbook)

    ☐ Create a new product listing with:

        ☐ A clear title (e.g. "Goal Getter Starter Pack")

        ☐ A bundled discount or added bonus to increase perceived value

    ☐ Update mockups and visuals in Canva

☐ Automate Delivery or Follow-Up Emails

    ☐ In your email platform (like MailerLite or ConvertKit), set up:

        ☐ A follow-up message with usage tips or a bonus download

        ☐ A simple thank-you email after purchase with links to other products

    ☐ Test it by signing up or purchasing as a customer would

☐ Brainstorm a Subscription or Digital Club Idea

Think about recurring value you could offer each month, such as:

- [ ] A new printable or template
- [ ] Exclusive prompts, art or writing challenges
- [ ] Behind-the-scenes videos, mini courses or a themed newsletter
- [ ] Write down 2–3 ideas and what would be included in each tier
- [ ] Create a System to Track Passive Offers
  - [ ] Set up a simple Airtable, Google Sheet, or Notion doc with:
    - [ ] Product name
    - [ ] Price point
    - [ ] Delivery method (Gumroad, Etsy, email, etc.)
    - [ ] Linked content or automations
      This helps you visualize and organize all your recurring income assets
- [ ] Update Your Link-in-Bio or Storefront
  - [ ] Make sure your bundles, evergreen offers or subscriptions are visible in your:
    - [ ] Instagram or TikTok bio
    - [ ] Linktree / Beacons / Carrd
    - [ ] Etsy or Gumroad homepage banner
  - [ ] Highlight them in your next few social posts

DAY 21: BONUS: REFLECT, CELEBRATE, AND PLAN WHAT'S NEXT

You made it. Seriously—look at everything you've done in just a few weeks. Most people think about starting. You started and kept going. That's worth celebrating.

Today is about stepping back to see how far you've come, checking in on what worked, what surprised you, and what you want to keep building.

Start by taking 5–10 minutes to reflect:

- What are you most proud of from this journey?
- Which days felt easiest or most fun?
- Which ones challenged you (in a good or tough way)?
- What's one small win you might've overlooked?

Write it down. Even if it's messy.

Now let's look at what's next.

You've got the tools. You've launched your first offer. You've started showing up as a brand and even built systems that let your work keep working—even when you're not actively posting.

That's not small. That's the foundation of a real business.

So here's the big question: where do you want to go from here?

You don't need a perfect roadmap. Just a direction. Think about what's feeling exciting right now:

- Launching a second product?
- Growing your email list?
- Testing a subscription idea?
- Leaning more into content, services or storytelling?

Set 1–2 goals for the next 30 days. Make them clear, doable, and tied to what you've already built. For example:

- "Write one blog post each week and link back to my Etsy shop".
- "Reach 100 email subscribers by offering a freebie".
- "Create 2 new listings by batching design work on Saturdays".

Keep it light, but keep it moving.

And finally—thank yourself.

You showed up. You learned. You created. That momentum is yours now.

PRACTICE: YOUR TURN

- Reflect on what you've built and how far you've come
- Set 1–2 small, clear goals for the next month
- Write down what's working—and what you'd like to try next
- Give yourself credit (and maybe a reward!)

WHAT YOU'VE LEARNED

You don't need to do everything at once. You just need a place to start, the willingness to try, and the tools to keep going. And now—you've got all three.

Whatever you build from here, you've proven you can figure it out.

Here's to what comes next.

DAY 21: REFLECT & PLAN CHECKLIST

- ☐ Write Down Your Biggest Win
  - ☐ What surprised you the most about what you accomplished?
  - ☐ Describe it in a sentence or two and keep it somewhere visible for motivation.
- ☐ Set 1–2 Specific Goals for the Next Month
  - ☐ Choose something actionable and measurable like, "Add 3 new listings to my shop", or "Start sending a monthly email newsletter" or "Earn my first $100 from digital products"
  - ☐ Write down the mini steps it'll take to hit each goal.
- ☐ List Tools or Strategies You'll Keep Using
  - ☐ Which AI tools, platforms, or systems made your life easier?
  - ☐ What workflows saved you time or gave you energy?
  - ☐ Note which ones you'll keep using weekly (e.g. Canva for mockups, ChatGPT for product ideas, MailerLite for email automation).
- ☐ Write a Short Reflection Entry
  - ☐ Jot down how you felt when you started vs. how you feel now.
  - ☐ Include a challenge you overcame and what helped you push through it. Even 5–6 sentences can help you acknowledge your growth and build momentum.
- ☐ Create a Monthly Content or Product Plan
  - ☐ Sketch out:
    - ☐ 2–3 social media post ideas
    - ☐ 1 new product concept or bundle idea

- [ ] 1 simple promotion or freebie
- [ ] Use your favorite calendar or planning tool to drop them into the next 4 weeks.
- [ ] Check In On Your Store or Platform Setup
  - [ ] Is your shop description up to date?
  - [ ] Are your links working (especially if you added Printify, MailerLite, etc.)?
  - [ ] Do you want to refresh your branding, visuals or pricing?
- [ ] Celebrate and Take a Break!
  - [ ] Mark the moment with a small reward—a treat, a walk, a post to share your milestone or just a good nap. You've built something real. Let it sink in.
  - [ ] Optional: Share your progress on social and invite others to follow your journey or check out your shop.

BONUS MATERIALS & WHAT'S NEXT

First off—if you've made it this far: I'm proud of you.

You've taken real steps toward building something on your own terms. This isn't the end of the road—it's a launchpad. And to make your next steps even easier, I've included a few extras for you.

BONUS 1: PRODUCT LAUNCH CHECKLIST (PRINTABLE)

Use this to plan your next product with clarity and confidence.

BONUS 2: QUICKSTART TOOL GUIDES

A short, skimmable guide to the tools we used in this book:

These are designed for when you're feeling stuck or just need a refresher without re-reading a whole chapter.

BONUS 3: CANVA QUICK GUIDE

WE WANT YOUR FEEDBACK

This book was built to be actionable, honest, and clear—and I'd love to hear how it felt for you.

- Did it help?
- Was anything confusing or unclear?
- Is there a specific chapter or topic you'd love to go deeper on?

Scan the QR code below to fill out a quick Google Form. You can:

- Share honest feedback (what worked, what didn't)
- Request additional material or a hands-on walkthrough
- Ask a question if you got stuck on something

If you want a direct reply, there's an optional field to leave your email. I won't send newsletters or promos—just a one-time reply to your question if needed.

LOVED IT? LEAVE A REVIEW

If this book helped you move forward, even a little—please consider leaving a short review on Amazon. It means the world to me and helps other creators find this resource when they need it most.

Thank you again for trusting me with your time, your energy, and your creative spark. This is just the beginning.

Keep building,

Tessa Quinn R.

Printed in Dunstable, United Kingdom

71225195R00103